Workers' Comp Management from A to Z
A "How To" Guide with Forms

Workers' Comp Management from A to Z

A "How To" Guide with Forms

Nancy Nivison Menzel, MS, RN, COHN

President, O·R·M Systems, Cambridge, Massachusetts
Formerly, President, Occupational Health Management,
Marion, Massachusetts, and Loss Management Coordinator,
Morton Hospital, Taunton, Massachusetts

OEM PRESS
Beverly, Massachusetts

ISBN 1-883595-01-0

Printed in the United States of America

Before implementing any component of the guidelines in this book, employers should first verify that it does not conflict with workers' compensation or labor laws that govern the organization.

To my children, Richard Andrew and Marianne Jean,
who are my finest accomplishments

Preface

This handbook is a practical guide for occupational health nurses and physicians, human resources professionals, safety directors, risk managers, workers' compensation coordinators, physical and occupational therapists, labor leaders, and anyone else concerned with reducing the frequency and severity of on-the-job injuries and illnesses and their detrimental effects and related costs. It is written in a straightforward style that makes even difficult concepts, such as the experience modification factor, easy to understand.

This guide to workers' compensation is intended to help readers understand the workers' comp system, identify problems having an adverse effect at their worksite, take steps to eliminate them, empower other employees to act innovatively, and limit the financial and human losses that do occur. The management system outlined in this book is a proven step-by-step approach to reducing workers' compensation losses. Many employers in both the public and private sectors have used these simple methods to reduce accident frequency and severity, lower premium costs, get more value from their insurance, support total quality improvement, and boost productivity.

Each component of the system is implemented through the use of forms, which are designed to be removed and photocopied onto the user's letterhead. The handbook includes a total of 37 practical, ready-to-use forms; for each form, a detailed explanation of its purpose and use appears on the lefthand facing page. The set of forms is also available on disk in WordPerfect 5.1/5.2 format (Windows or DOS), which will enable rapid customization for use in a particular organization. (See the order form at the back of the book.)

Through this "win-win" loss-control system, workers will also benefit through increased job security due to a healthier bottom line, effective safety programs, and protection from work-related injuries and illnesses. This system will limit opportunities for abuse or malingering, which is now estimated to be a factor in up to 25% of all workers' comp claims in some areas of the country.

There are as many different workers' compensation and labor laws in the United States as there are states and jurisdictions. Because of the variety and complexity of these laws, this book is intended to be a general overview and is therefore not specific to each state, jurisdiction, or type of coverage. Before implementing any component of this system, employers should first verify that it does not conflict with workers' compensation or labor laws that govern the organization.

If this book helps to prevent even one accident or to return an injured employee to work sooner than usual, it will have paid for itself. If a company restructures its procedures to incorporate this loss-control system, it will be able to focus more attention on its main business, while its employees will be able to work more productively in a safer environment.

I am grateful for the valuable contributions of the two occupational health professionals and the workers' comp insurance advisor who provided chapters for this book: John A. Davis, MD, Martin Goldenberg, LIA, and Patti E. Walkover, MS, RN.

My thanks also to A. Vincent DeRobbio, MD, who has encouraged me in my efforts to assist injured workers and their employers. In serving these two "masters," he walks a fine line with both compassion and practicality.

I am grateful to the many employees and employers with whom I have worked over the years. My experiences with them have given me the rich material for the examples in this book. They have taught me again and again that the only truly "successful" workers' comp case is the one that is prevented. If an employee does become injured or ill on the job, the next best outcome is rehabilitation and return to work. No one wins when an injury or illness is career-ending, regardless of the size of the final settlement.

N.N.M.

Contributors

John A. Davis, MD, is board-certified in internal medicine, occupational medicine, and addiction medicine. He is past president of the New England Occupational Medicine Association and current member of the House of Delegates for the American College of Occupational and Environmental Medicine. He is a member of the impartial panel of the Massachusetts Department of Industrial Accidents and medical advisor to Tufts Managed Comp. He speaks locally and nationally on medical build-up in disability claims.

Dr. Davis was formerly Chief of Occupational Medicine for Neponset Valley Occupational Medicine. In 1991, he founded Davis Occupational Medicine in Norwood, Massachusetts, which serves approximately 200 corporate clients. Dr. Davis is currently president of the organization.

Martin Goldenberg, LIA, is a licensed insurance advisor with over 35 years' experience as an insurance agent and broker. In 1991, he formed the Workers' Compensation Consulting Group in Boston, Massachusetts, which specializes in assisting clients throughout the country in developing and monitoring their workers' compensation insurance and cost-control programs.

He addresses such issues as investigation of alternatives to standard insurance policies, reviewing for accuracy the experience modification factor computation, proper code classification, policy audit results, and correct application of rating organization rules and regulations.

Mr. Goldenberg believes that employers often blindly accept their regular premium increases as a fact of life, whereas they could be saving substantial premium dollars by knowing and applying to their situation all the procedures and intricacies of the workers' compensation system.

Nancy Nivison Menzel, MS, RN, COHN, holds a BS in nursing from Cornell University, an MA in administration from Columbia University, and MS degrees in physiology and occupational health from Boston University and the Harvard University School of Public Health. She has worked in health care for 30 years, devoting the last 15 years to occupational health, with specialization in workplace safety and workers' compensation loss-control programs in a variety of settings. Today, she is president of O R M Systems, Inc., an occupational health and safety company in Cambridge, Massachusetts.

Patti E. Walkover, MS, RN, is Director of Occupational Health and Workers' Comp Managed Care for VHA East in Berwin, Pennsylvania, where she developed a regional workers' comp managed-care program with a network of 17 occupational health specialty centers. Following a 50% increase in workers' comp insurance rates in Pennsylvania, this managed-care program was established to provide lower cost, higher quality care than traditional methods of service delivery.

The managed-care program provides a range of services, including utilization management, precertification (approval for services prior to delivery), access to an integrated provider network, and case management. VHA East is expanding the managed-care program to neighboring states.

Ms. Walkover has a master's degree in occupational health from the Harvard School of Public Health and has had extensive experience managing hospital-based occupational health programs and establishing workers' comp control systems for employers.

Contents

1

Understanding and Controlling Workers' Comp Costs

Nancy Nivison Menzel, MS, RN, COHN, and Martin Goldenberg, LIA

In today's national and global economy, more and more businesses are finding it difficult to compete against rivals with lower labor costs. One factor that influences the cost of labor is workers' compensation insurance, which escalated rapidly in many states before recently leveling off in response to a variety of control measures. To guard against future cost escalations and to get out and stay out of the expensive high-risk pool, employers must head off workers' comp problems through creative approaches.

Managers waiting for legislative reform to limit potential losses may be out of business long before the legislators begin their deliberations. Companies must administer their workers' comp program effectively under existing rules, just as they now do for taxation, general disability insurance, pension funds, and other costs of doing business.

Understanding the History of Workers' Comp Laws

The industrial revolution brought with it high-speed machinery, an end to slow production methods, and unsafe work conditions, all of which produced large increases in work-related injuries and illnesses. Injured or ill employees had no system to provide for wages or medical care other than suing their employers for not meeting their common-law obligations to the employee, which are a safe workplace, an adequate number of co-workers, safe equipment, effective safety programs, and clear warnings of work-related dangers.

Employees rarely won these suits against their employers. By the late 1880s, a reform movement brought about changes in the way employees with work-related injuries or illnesses could receive coverage for medical expenses and lost wages.

In 1897, England enacted a workers' comp law that was based on the concept of no fault, in which neither party had to prove negligence. In 1911, Wisconsin passed the first U.S. workers' comp law that was found to be constitutional; other states soon followed its example. Today, all 50 states and U.S. possessions have workers' comp laws, but all vary to some degree in their coverages and provisions.

The basic objectives of workers' comp laws are:

- To offer prompt income and medical benefits.
- To provide a single remedy, that is, to exclude further law suits related to the injury or illness, between employer and employee.
- To allow businesses, not charities or general health insurance, to absorb the cost of injuries.
- To reduce legal costs and delays.
- To encourage safety by rewarding (through premium adjustments) employers with good accident records and penalize those with poor records.
- To allow more accurate investigation and prevention by removing a party's motivation to conceal the facts to avoid negligence charges.

What Does Workers' Comp Cost the Nation?

Estimates of the annual U. S. costs of workers' comp exceed $60 billion. This number seems so high that it is nearly meaningless. However, each employer bears part of this burden and must add the cost of workers' comp insurance to the cost of its goods and services.

Example A sandwich-shop chain paying $3,000 per employee annually in workers' comp premium has to charge more for its submarine sandwiches than a competitor who pays only $500 per employee.

Workers' comp insurance is an overhead expense that does not increase productivity or add value. Much of the money paid for workers' comp insurance does not go directly to the injured or ill employee. (Worker's comp policies refer to work-related illnesses as occupational diseases.) It is eaten up by administrative costs (for adjusters, agents, auditors, plan administrators, and others). Employers should have as their goal getting their costs as low as possible through a variety of the effective techniques described in this book.

Managing Workers' Comp Costs

Form 1-1, **Overview of Effective Workers' Comp Loss Control Measures,** is a summary of the steps an organization must take to ensure that it is providing a safe workplace, adequate medical care, and effective case management. Use it as a guide to improve your organization's workers' comp cost-control approaches.

Source of Further Information

WCRI Research Brief. Periodical that (according to masthead) "reports on significant ideas, issues, research studies, and data of interest to those working to better understand and to improve workers' compensation systems." Published by the Workers' Compensation Research Institute, 101 Main Street, Cambridge, MA 02142; tel. (617) 494-1240.

Form 1-1, Overview of Effective Workers' Comp Loss-Control Measures

Purpose of Form

- To serve as an introduction to the steps that must be taken to achieve control of workers' comp losses
- To provide a checklist to mark progress in completing steps

Use of Form

- Management should review the steps and assign responsibility for achieving them.
- When a step has been achieved, check it off.

Form 1-1

OVERVIEW OF EFFECTIVE WORKERS' COMP LOSS-CONTROL MEASURES

Administrative Controls

☐ Review insurance coverage for appropriateness and cost-saving possibilities.

☐ Obtain help from insurance carrier or agent, if applicable.

☐ Establish minimum standards for carrier's or third-party administrator's performance.

☐ Review program periodically for hallmarks of success: reduced costs, reduced accidents, reduced severity.

Risk Reduction

☐ Establish safety committee and programs.

☐ Complete hazard evaluation.

☐ Initiate safety self-inspection process with periodic reports.

☐ Plan ways to reduce hazards and improve safety.

☐ Adopt health and safety policy statement, code of safe practices, and injured-worker policies.

☐ Orient new employees to safety policies, procedures, and disciplinary actions.

☐ Establish preplacement medical exams.

☐ Implement accident reporting and investigation.

☐ Establish incident/hazard reporting system.

☐ Compile OSHA Incidence and Severity Rates monthly.

☐ Management involvement:

- Meet with employees to discuss safety program, goals.
- Review accident/incident reports and investigations.
- Incorporate incidence data into periodic management reporting.
- Begin safety incentive program.

Post-Injury Response

- ☐ Select qualified health-care providers.
- ☐ Train supervisors on post-injury response.
- ☐ Appoint workers' compensation coordinator (WCC).
- ☐ Provide case management for all work injuries and illnesses.
- ☐ Contact employee, supervisor, adjuster, health-care provider.
- ☐ Review cases for possibility of fraud or malingering.
- ☐ Achieve case-management goal of returning the employee to work and reducing associated costs of the claim.

Early Return to Work

- ☐ Write company policy supporting return to work in modified duty.
- ☐ Obtain collective bargaining agreement (if needed) to allow modified duty.
- ☐ Develop system for basing modified-duty assignments on abilities and restrictions.
- ☐ Train supervisors in implementation of modified duty.
- ☐ Offer modified duty to injured/ill employees who are medically cleared.
- ☐ Return employees to time-limited modified-duty positions.
- ☐ Close cases as rapidly as possible.

2

Types of Workers' Comp Policies

Martin Goldenberg, LIA

Buying Standard Workers' Comp Insurance Policies

In 1992, the National Council on Compensation Insurance (NCCI), an industry-sponsored nonprofit organization that functions as an administrator to the workers' compensation insurance system in 37 states and the District of Columbia, revised its standard workers' comp and employers' liability policy to incorporate state-specific requirements and to simplify the language used. This standard policy is customized to each state by means of endorsements that conform to its particular laws. The NCCI policy is used in all the states (including those for which it does not act as an administrator) and the District of Columbia, with the exception of Nevada, North Dakota, Ohio, Washington, West Virginia, and Wyoming. These six states are so-called monopolistic states, which run their own insurance programs.

Workers' comp insurance can be purchased from insurance carriers, state funds, or self-insured groups, or (if you qualify) you can self-insure. The majority of businesses buy their coverage from insurance companies, either through the voluntary (competitive) market or the so-called residual market (assigned risk).

The assigned risk plan was developed to cover employers that cannot purchase workers' comp insurance in the voluntary market due to an unfavorable loss record or other factors. Since workers' comp coverage is mandated by most state laws, each jurisdiction has established a procedure to provide insurance to those who cannot obtain coverage in the open market. Assigned-risk insurance policies are the same as those obtained in the voluntary market, but the application process is different and the rates are usually higher due to surcharges.

The cost of workers' compensation insurance has been increasing rampantly throughout the country for the past 10 years, with minor exceptions. Some states have passed workers' comp reform legislation, which is starting to reduce the size of claim payments and to result in premium decreases.

> **Example** Massachusetts passed reform legislation in December 1991, and by January 1994, it had reduced insurance rates by an average of 10.24%. While most rates went down, a few went up. For example, an employer previously paying $.39 per $100 of payroll for clerical employees is now charged $.33 per $100, a 15% decrease. However, the rate for boilermakers increased 13%, from $14.96 to $16.96 per $100 of payroll.

This chapter gives a brief description of the various plans that are available. It is important to remember that economic conditions, rules, regulations, and insurance companies' underwriting requirements vary in each state. *Underwriting requirements* are the criteria used by an insurance company to make a final decision on whether to provide insurance to a specific company or to refuse to issue a policy. These requirements include factors such as size of the premium, past experience, and claim history, to name a few. All of these have an impact on how employers purchase their policies. (Form 2-1, **Workers' Comp Insurance Needs Evaluation**, can be used to assess an organization's needs.)

Where to Purchase Workers' Comp Insurance

Insurance Companies/Carriers

These are the basic providers of workers' compensation insurance. The policy form is standard as to coverage and does not differ among companies. However, carriers do offer different types of premium basis, such as guaranteed cost, retrospective rating, or large deductibles, which are explained in a subsequent section of this chapter.

State Funds

These are established in the same manner as an insurance company, but are under control of the state. Some states operate funds that compete with the insurance companies. However, the states of Nevada, North Dakota, Ohio, Washington, West Virginia, and Wyoming run monopolistic state funds, which means they are the only market for the purchase of workers' comp insurance. Their coverage is only applicable in the particular state. If you operate in multiple states, you must purchase insurance to cover the exposure in each state. This could mean having several policies.

Self-Insurance Groups

Self-insurance groups (SIGs) are usually associations of homogeneous companies that band together to pool both premiums and losses. Typically, SIGs consist of hospitals, nursing homes, manufacturers, and retailers. The ultimate objective is to reduce each member's costs by a dividend that results from efficient operation of the pool, control of claims administration, and provision of effective engineering (loss control) services. Policy forms are the same as those of an insurance carrier.

The *disadvantage* of a self-insurance group is that the members are jointly and severally liable, which means that the financial strength of the group depends on its members. If one member has a financial problem, it could be shared by the rest of the group.

The main *advantage* of a SIG is the possibility for premium savings.

Example Several hospitals formed a self-insured group that refunded 25% of all premiums paid to its members after its fourth year of operation.

Self-Insurance

Each state has rules and regulations that control whether or not a business can be self-insured. If your organization meets the requirements, you provide coverage in the same manner as an insurance company. Instead of paying premiums to an insurance company, you use the same dollars to provide all services and pay claims. The requirements to become self-insured vary; for example, in the state of Massachusetts employers need to meet the following criteria before making an application:

- Minimum of 300 employees
- Standard premium of at least $750,000
- Experience modification factor not in excess of 1.25
- A Standard and Poor's rating of AA or a Dun & Bradstreet rating of 5A
- A surety bond of at least $1,000,000
- Audited financial statements that show a profit for the last 3 years

If an employer meets these requirements, it may then apply to become a self-insurer, subject to the approval of the Massachusetts Department of Industrial Accidents.

Types of Policies

These are the two basic ways to purchase workers' comp insurance: guaranteed cost and retrospective rating. Regardless of how the insurance policy is structured, employers can fine tune the size of the premium through the use of deductibles.

Guaranteed Cost

Premium is based on the class-code rate (assigned by the insurance company to describe the business, such as bottle manufacturer or automobile dealership) multiplied by the payroll (estimated payroll dollars assigned to this code) multiplied by the experience modification factor less any premium discounts. Premium discounts are available in proportion to the size of the premium and vary by state. No other factors are involved in guaranteed-cost insurance; thus, employers can predict premium costs in advance. (Some states do apply a surcharge for employers in the assigned-risk category or for those with worse-than-average losses.) This type of premium is most common, as it allows sound budgeting and is not subject to large swings in premium, except for cases in which the payroll was underestimated at policy inception. All workers' comp policies are subject to auditing when they expire, and it is only then that organizations can get an accurate cost.

DEDUCTIBLES (SMALL OR LARGE)

Deductibles are becoming more popular and provide an insured with a method that may help control rising workers' comp costs. Small-deductible plans are standard and are controlled by NCCI or state workers' comp rating organizations. Large-deductible plans vary in size and operation and are filed by individual insurers for approval by their rating organization.

Small deductibles can run from $100 to $10,000 and cover medical and/or indemnity claims. The allowed premium credit ranges from 0.6% to 26%. The insurance carrier usually pays the claim in full and then asks for reimbursement from the insured. It is important to clarify whether or not the deductible amount will be included or excluded when the insurance carrier reports claim values to the workers' comp rating organization. If they are excluded from reporting, it will have a positive effect on the experience modification factor. However, if they are included in reporting, it will have a double-negative effect, as the insured both pays the deductible out of pocket and is charged for it in the experience-rating plan.

Before deciding on a deductible plan, you should consider the number of claims normally incurred, the total out-of-pocket cost, and how the payments are factored into the experience-rating plan. Since the deductible is per claim, and frequency of claims has a large impact on the net cost, you should have your insurance agent or a consultant do a cost comparison before purchasing a deductible plan.

Large-deductible plans are not available in every state and are not appropriate for many organizations. A large-deductible plan is a good choice if your organization is considering self-insurance but is still uneasy about the ultimate net effect of retrospective rating or self-insurance. These plans can start with a minimum deductible of $100,000 and a premium of at least $500,000. If your state allows large-deductible plans, the terms are usually negotiated with the insurance carrier and the rating organization. Some of the advantages are a reduction in cash flow, the advantages of self-insurance without the disadvantages, and an incentive for implementing and monitoring loss-control programs.

Retrospective Rating

The standard premium is based on class-code rates multiplied by $100 of payroll multiplied by the experience modification factor without a premium discount. A retrospective rating plan is then applied on top of the guaranteed-cost premium. There are various "retro" formulas that can be applied, and they all work on the principal of a basic premium (fixed charge) plus converted losses multiplied by a tax factor. (Converted losses are the actual cost of the claim marked up to cover administrative expenses.) The final retro calculation is subject to a maximum and a minimum premium. It gives organizations an opportunity to reduce their insurance costs if they control their claims. However, if they are not successful, they may pay an extra premium.

Retrospective rating is designed for businesses that have large guaranteed-cost premiums. There is no magic premium level to justify venturing into a retrospective rating plan, but $500,000 appears to be a reasonable minimum, along with the presence of a strong safety program.

Premium Computations

The premium of a workers' compensation policy is broken into two sections. The basic charge is the dollar amount per $100 of payroll multiplied by the rate applicable to the code assigned to the payroll. For example, $100,000 payroll for clerical workers with a rate of $.30 per hundred results in a $300 premium charge.

The *class codes* are standards that have been developed by NCCI to describe various business operations. While there are over 600 codes, it is obvious that there is not an exact code for every type of business. The appropriate workers' comp rating organization determines the code that is most applicable. If you disagree, you can appeal the decision and request a hearing for a redetermination by the rating bureau, and if still not satisfied, you can make an appeal to the insurance department of your state. Usually, the original class determination is made without an inspection, which may result in an inaccurate description of the business operation.

> **Example** A helicopter medical-evacuation service was incorrectly rated in a class that carried a much higher rate per dollar of payroll than its correct classification. The company appealed the rating bureau's determination and was successful in lowering its class code.

The codes are standard, with some exceptions, but the rates vary between jurisdictions. The rates are based on claim dollars paid and reserved plus expenses as they relate to premium dollars collected. Each insurance company is required to report this information to the workers' comp rating authority. The rate that is promulgated becomes the starting point for the experience modification factor (EMF).

Experience rating combines your past claim and premium history to predict your future losses. This figure is then compared to expected losses for similar-size businesses within your state. If you are above average, a debit results, and if you are below average, a credit is the result. The EMF is referred to in relationship to 1.0 (unity). An example of a debit mod would be 1.15, or a 15% surcharge on the rate, and an example of a credit mod would be .80, or a 20% reduction on the rate. To explain the EMF formula in detail is beyond the scope of this book. Stated simply, it would look like this fraction:

$$\frac{\text{Actual primary losses} + \text{Stabilizing value} + \text{Ratable excess}}{\text{Expected primary losses} + \text{Stabilizing value} + \text{Ratable excess}} = \text{EMF}$$

Example

	PRIMARY LOSSES	STABILIZING VALUE	RATABLE EXCESS	TOTALS
ACTUAL	26,500	75,000	15,000	116,500 (J)
EXPECTED	20,000	75,000	9,500	104,500 (K)

EXPERIENCE MODIFICATION

(J)/(K)
1.12

Elements of the formula:

- Actual primary losses are the full amount of paid and reserve dollars, up to $5,000.

- Expected primary losses are the dollars that you are expected to have based on your payroll size, up to $5,000.

- Stabilizing values are figures put into the formula to account for size.

- Ratable excess is the amount of claim over $5,000 that goes into the formula. The first $5,000 of any claim is considered at full value and anything over that is cushioned within the formula.

- The information used in the formula consists of audited payroll and losses, including the total of paid and reserved amounts for a 3-year period starting 4 years prior to the current effective date. For example, a policy effective January 1, 1994, is based on payroll and losses for the 3 policy years of January 1, 1990, to January 1, 1993.

Experience rating is the cornerstone of the workers' comp system and is the reason that you must follow all the loss-prevention and claim-management recommendations in this book to lower your premium. The formula is complicated, but this overview illustrates its principles and how it affects your premium. When you receive your workers' comp experience-modification computation, review it for accuracy using Form 2-2, **Experience Modification Checklist**.

Source of Further Information

ABCs of Revised Experience Rating. National Council on Compensation Insurance, 750 Park of Commerce Drive, Boca Raton, FL 33487-3621. (Available at a nominal cost.)

Scopes of Basic Manual Classifications. National Council on Compensation Insurance, 750 Park of Commerce Drive, Boca Raton, FL 33487-3621.

Form 2-1, Workers' Comp Insurance Needs Evaluation

Purpose of Form

- To perform a self-evaluation of workers' comp needs
- To make sure an organization has purchased workers' comp insurance that is adequate for its needs

Use of Form

- Complete the questionnaire annually.
- Review answers with an insurance agent, insurance broker, or insurance advisor to ensure that the organization has adequate workers' comp insurance coverage.

Form 2-1

WORKERS' COMP INSURANCE NEEDS EVALUATION

1. Do your employees work in more than one state? _____

2. Do you have specific job locations in states other than your home state? _____

3. Do you operate in any of the monopolistic states or jurisdictions?

    NV___   ND___   OH___   WA___   WV___   WY___   PR___   CAN___

4. Do you have any work exposures on, or adjacent to, navigable waters? _____

5. Do you hire leased employees? _____

6. Do you hire independent contractors on a regular basis? _____

7. Do you hire minors or illegal immigrants? _____

8. Do you provide recreational facilities or sponsor sport activities? _____

9. Do you have a workers' comp coordinator? _____

10. Is your workers' comp insurance obtained from the assigned risk pool? _____
    Is it part of a group plan? _____

11. Who is your present workers' comp carrier? _____

12. What is the workers' comp insurance premium? _____

13. What is your experience modification factor? _____

14. What surcharges (e.g., ARAP) do you pay? _____

15. Do you have a retrospective rating plan policy? _____

16. Do you have a participating dividend plan policy? _____

17. Does your NCCI class code accurately describe your business? _____

Workers' Comp Management from A to Z: A "How to" Guide with Forms. © Nancy Nivison Menzel, OEM Press, Beverly, MA, 1994.

Form 2-2, Experience Modification Checklist

Purpose of Form

- To check the validity of the experience modification calculation provided by the workers' comp rating bureau
- To ensure that the organization is not being overcharged for its workers' comp insurance due to an erroneous experience modification factor

Use of Form

- Ask the insurance agent, broker, or consultant for assistance in obtaining a copy of the organization's most recent calculation of the experience modification factor.
- Review the formula using the items on the checklist.
- Notify the insurance agent, broker, consultant, or workers' comp rating bureau of any errors discovered.
- Follow this procedure annually.

Form 2-2

EXPERIENCE MODIFICATION CHECKLIST

1. Do the payrolls on the experience modification worksheet match the payrolls by class from the final policy audit for the 3 applicable years?

2. Does workers' comp loss information from the appropriate loss run from the insurance carrier match the amounts shown by claim number and loss amounts, both paid and reserved?

3. Are there any duplicate claim entries?

4. Are all the claims yours?

5. Ask your insurance agent or consultant to verify that the formula is correct and is correctly computed.

3

Ways Your Insurance Company and Agent Can Work for You

Nancy Nivison Menzel, MS, RN, COHN, and Martin Goldenberg, LIA

How Workers' Comp Carriers, Brokers, Agents, and Consultants Can Help Your Organization

When you purchase a workers' comp insurance policy, you are buying more than a piece of paper. It is a contract between you and the insurance company, and each side has certain obligations to the other. We all know that the insurance company pays the legal obligations of claims, but in addition to that responsibility, they can and should provide some other important services to their policy holders.

Organizations should consider insurance brokers and agents as potential sources of assistance as well. An insurance *agent* represents one or many insurance companies and has the authority to write insurance policies that are binding on a carrier. Some carriers do not authorize any agents.

An insurance *broker* has no authority to represent a particular carrier. Brokers are licensed by the state and act as intermediaries between clients and insurance carriers. A broker assists clients in determining their insurance needs and then seeks a carrier willing to insure the risks. Brokers may receive either a percentage of the premium as a commission or may charge a flat service fee.

After drawing upon these available resources, organizations may still feel the need to hire an insurance advisor to evaluate their workers' comp insurance needs. A *licensed insurance advisor* (LIA) is licensed by a state to act as an independent consultant on insurance matters. An LIA does not represent a specific insurance company or sell policies.

Before deciding whether to use a broker, agent, or insurance advisor, ask them to explain their credentials and what services they will provide an organization. At a minimum, any broker or agent selling workers' comp insurance should understand the state's workers' comp law, the experience rating system, and the suitability, advantages, and disadvantages of the types of workers' comp insurance coverage available. In addition, insurance advisors should demonstrate competence at selecting cost-effective insurance coverage for the organization, while not leaving it exposed to uninsured losses.

Services Your Insurance Carrier Provides

Insurance companies employ full-time engineers, nurses, and safety specialists whose job it is to assist clients in loss-control activities, sometimes called *engineering services*. Upon request, they will provide safety inspections and make recommendations to eliminate hazardous conditions that could cause accidents and injuries. Appendix A contains a sample loss-control report written by an insurance carrier's safety engineer.

In addition to these walk-through inspections, carriers' loss-control staff may also survey areas for hazardous noise levels, monitor the air for hazardous chemical exposures, and provide advice on regulatory compliance programs. Organizations should request that the carrier provide these services on a regular basis; for example, quarterly, semiannually, or annually.

Insurance companies do not represent that their engineering services will keep you in compliance with OSHA or other regulations. In addition, the quality of these services varies from carrier to carrier. If the organization is in the voluntary market and has a choice of workers' comp carriers, it should evaluate the quality of each carrier's engineering services. Ask to review a sample loss-control report and for a description of other services provided.

Upon a client's request, carriers will provide periodic summaries of claim activity. These periodic reports are called *loss runs* and are explained in greater detail in Chapter 21. In general, loss runs contain information on the claim number, the date and type of injury or illness, the amounts paid for medical care or wage replacement, and dollar estimates (*reserves*) of how much the claim is predicted to cost before it is closed. Loss runs assist organizations in managing their workers' comp cases and in controlling costs.

Another service that carriers provide their clients is coordination of all claim activity by a supervisor who is familiar with the insured organization's work environment and modified-duty policies. An organization's workers' comp coordinator should be able to develop a good working relationship with a carrier's claims supervisor through regular contact and communication.

The insurance company updates an organization's payroll and claim information by submitting it to the appropriate workers' comp rating bureau on unit statistical cards, commonly called *"unit stat cards."* Using this information, the rating bureau promulgates an organization's experience modification factor, which is why an organization should ensure that all information on unit stat cards is accurate and up to date.

The insurance carrier submits unit stat cards 6 months after the expiration of a policy and every 12 months thereafter. It is important for an organization to meet with the claim supervisor *prior to* these deadlines to try to close claims and set reserves at proper levels.

Services Your Broker or Agent Provides

In addition to helping an organization select cost-effective workers' comp insurance coverage, both brokers and agents should help their clients prepare for the workers' comp audit. All comp policies are written with an estimated payroll that is subject to final audit to determine the actual premium. The insurance auditor will send notification of the audit date, allowing an organization to prepare in advance with the help of a broker or agent. Form 3-1, **Preparation for a Workers' Comp Audit,** outlines the information an organization should review and actions it should take prior to the audit. Form 3-2, **Workers' Comp Audit Checklist**, provides items to scrutinize carefully to guard against overcharging.

Services a Licensed Insurance Advisor Provides

Workers' comp insurance is a specialized area with complicated and changing regulations and provisions. Employers sometimes engage the services of an insurance advisor to assist them in reviewing insurance alternatives and offer advice on buying correct coverage, recovering past overpayments, and ensuring that the organization is not overcharged.

> **Example** A gas-and-electric utility with 100 employees was paying $125,000 in workers' comp premiums annually. An insurance advisor reviewed payroll information and found that clerical and management employees had been misclassified as installation and repair workers. By reclassifying these employees to the correct codes, the utility recouped $50,000 for past overcharges and lowered future premium expenses.

An insurance advisor can also explain other ways to save workers' comp insurance costs and reduce risks.

Example An insurance advisor observed that most workers' comp claims made by the employees of a nursing home came from the employees who worked in the kitchen. Since food service was not its main line of business, the nursing home subcontracted this ancillary service to an outside vendor, who was then responsible for the kitchen employees' workers' comp insurance costs.

Advisors also educate organizations on ways to minimize risks, such as ensuring that outside contractors present evidence of workers' comp insurance. Without such insurance, an organization may be liable for any work-related injuries or illnesses that occur to employees of these contractors.

Employers who directly hire temporary workers assume responsibility for their workers' comp coverage. Employers can avoid this risk by hiring short-term workers through a temporary agency that provides workers' comp insurance for its employees.

Example A document-scanning company hired temporary employees to perform low-skill tasks. The second day on the job, a female temporary employee hurried outside to buy something from a snack-vendor's truck and fell on ice in the parking lot, fracturing her skull. The employer was liable for the extremely expensive workers' comp claim that resulted, even though the company did not consider the woman a "regular" employee.

Form 3-1, Preparation for a Workers' Comp Audit

Purpose of the Form

- To allow the organization time to gather all the information the insurance auditor will request
- To provide an opportunity for the organization to review the information for accuracy
- To maximize the chances of getting an accurate audit

Use of the Form

- When notified of the date of the audit, complete the recommended steps.
- Call the insurance agent, broker, or advisor and request their attendance at the audit, along with the organization's workers' comp coordinator.
- Have the prepared information available on the day of the audit.

Form 3-1

PREPARATION FOR A WORKERS' COMP AUDIT

1. Break your payroll down by worker's comp class codes. The basis of a premium is *all* remuneration, which consists of wages, bonuses, commissions, overtime pay, holiday pay, vacation pay, sick-day pay, and contributions to IRAs. (Convert overtime pay to straight time.)

2. Make sure the payrolls conform with quarterly tax returns.

3. Reduce executive officers' payroll amounts to individual state limits.

4. If you have payroll in more than one state, break it down by state and workers' comp class codes, as rates vary by state.

5. Have certificates of insurance from all subcontractors available for the auditor to verify. If certificates are not present, you can be charged for monies paid to subcontractors based on their workers' comp class code.

6. Have the auditor leave a copy of his or her worksheets, so that you can use it to check against the final billing.

Workers' Comp Management from A to Z: A "How to" Guide with Forms. © Nancy Nivison Menzel, OEM Press, Beverly, MA, 1994.

Form 3-2, Workers' Comp Audit Checklist

Purpose of the Form

- To provide benchmarks for the audit process
- To assist employers in obtaining an accurate audit

Use of the Form

- All questions should be answered with a "yes" to verify accuracy of the audit.
- Ask for clarification of any audit actions that appear confusing or incorrect, such as an auditor disagreeing with how payrolls are classified.

Form 3-2

WORKERS' COMP AUDIT CHECKLIST

1. Has the proper payroll been assigned to the correct classification codes?

2. Have all applicable payroll limitations rules been applied?

   a. Executive officers' pay may have state limits.

   b. All overtime converted to straight time

3. Have the proper rates been charged for the corresponding classification codes?

4. Has the proper premium discount been applied?

5. Has the correct experience modification factor been applied?

6. Has the correct ARAP surcharge been applied, if applicable?

7. If more than one state is covered, has the payroll been assigned to the correct states? This is important, as the rates for each state are different.

8. Check audit billing against the copy of the audit worksheet, which you retained from the actual audit.

9. Check all mathematical calculations for accuracy.

4

Establishing a Safety Program and Committee

Does your company have a strong corporate safety program? Does top management demand that safety be incorporated as part of its drive for excellence? Does it have an effective safety committee? Does it have at least one employee designated as responsible for safety? If the answer is "no" to any of these questions, your company is probably experiencing an excessive number of accidents, has high insurance costs, and copes with adversarial relationships with employees, who are suffering unnecessary injuries and illnesses.

Safety Program

The main difference between companies that reduce accidents and those that don't is the strength of their safety programs. Safety programs are organized ways of ensuring both safe workplaces and safe work practices. The best programs are characterized by strong management commitment and leadership, with employee involvement expected and demanded throughout the organization. If management sends a message that safety is just something to appease regulators and not a tool to improve excellence, employees will reluctantly and inconsistently participate in programs.

Practical tip The chief executive officer (CEO) should also be the chief safety officer and should demand the same progressive approaches to safety as to other company capabilities. This designation serves as a daily reminder to both the CEO and employees that management is involved in safety.

Plastering the premises with safety slogans will have no effect if the CEO withholds money for needed safety improvements or training. Management teams reluctant to devote resources to improving safety programs can sometimes be persuaded to invest in safety by pointing out that employees who are working safely are also working more efficiently and productively.

Example One company had numerous back injuries in an area where employees had to lift heavy boxes from the floor to a 4-foot-high surface. Management refused to buy special spring-supported pallets that rise as they are unloaded, until the consultant pointed out how much faster employees could work by eliminating the steps of turning, stooping, lifting, pivoting, and unloading. The new pallets arrived within days.

Minimal elements of a safety program include:

- Involvement of management
- Involvement of employees
- Adequate safety budget
- Regulatory compliance program
- Written safety policies and procedures
- Employee training during regular work hours
- Required safe work practices
- Established safety committee
- Appointed safety director
- Accidents recorded, reported, and investigated
- Safety statistics analyzed and compared with benchmarks
- Safety audits and inspections

Workplace safety is a specialized field that includes many credentialed safety professionals, vast libraries of safety materials, proprietary safety systems, and warehouses full of protective gear, from ear plugs to fall arrest systems. With these resources available, no company can use the excuse that it "just doesn't know" how to have a safer workplace. To find out how your safety program stacks up, grade it with the **Safety-Program Report Card** (Form 4-1).

Safety Director

On every premises, there should be one individual designated as safety director. In smaller facilities, this person may wear many hats and devote only small amounts of time to safety. In larger facilities, there is often a full-time safety director who may also have full-time assistants. Whatever the structure, one individual should have both responsibility and authority for site safety.

Safety Committee

Any safety program needs a safety committee to accomplish its goal of reduced accidents. These committees, which should be made up of both management and hourly workers, are a vehicle to ensure employee involvement in recognizing and abating hazards and implementing changes acceptable to others because the suggestions come from peers and tend to be practical. If the company has a medical department, a nurse or physician should also participate.

Organizing the Committee

There are six things to decide about safety committees: size, number, membership, meeting frequency, purpose, and authority. (See Form 4-2, **Safety-Committee Report Card**.)

1. **Size** Committees with over 15 members will find discussions slow and difficult, with many members holding back from participation. *Strive for smaller, more agile committees.*

2. **Number** If the company is very large, with diverse processes and activities, it is best to have numerous small committees. These committees can be organized by location (e.g., Mill Street plant, North River plant), by activity (e.g., residential treatment programs); by hazard (e.g., radiation safety); by purpose (e.g., ergonomic safety); or by working hours (e.g., night-shift safety). If the company is small or not varied in its components, one committee may be adequate.

3. **Membership** An even mix of supervisors and hourly employees should make up the committee, with 2- or 3-year terms that expire at different times to ensure continuity. Most committees are made up of volunteers. Be sure to include someone from the medical department or the first-responder team.

4. **Meetings** Management should set aside time during regular working hours for meetings. Committees should meet on a regularly scheduled basis—at least monthly. In settings with many accidents, the committee might meet weekly until the hazards are abated.

5. **Purpose** Committees should draw up a statement of purpose that identifies goals, responsibilities, and activities. These could include employee accident investigation, training programs, safety inspections, early intervention programs, and employee/management communication.

6. **Authority** Management should clearly define the committee's authority. Does it have the authority to establish policies and procedures? Will it have a budget that it controls? May it issue its recommendations directly to involved departments? The more authority the committee has, the more effective it will be.

> **Example** A company reported that it could not maintain an effective safety committee because meeting attendance kept declining. The consultant found that the committee was scheduled to meet after normal working hours and had no authority. (It had submitted its early findings to the president, who read and filed them without implementation.) When the meeting time was reset to normal working hours and the committee given authority to implement change, participation increased.

Giving the safety committee a *budget* helps to increase its authority and promotes respect from the other employees. The committee should identify needs, prepare a budget request, and carefully compare dollars requested with projected savings (cost/benefit analysis).

> **Example** The safety committee at an electronics manufacturer requested $10,000 for a series of chemical-safety training programs. The company had been fined $35,000 by OSHA for failing to provide such training to several employees who had been injured in a hydrofluoric acid spill. The accident had also caused an increase in workers' comp costs and production interruptions. The committee received its requested money after it demonstrated that the training sessions would prevent such accidents and the associated human and financial costs in the future.

Focus of the Committee

The safety committee should focus on preventing or reducing the severity of workplace injuries and illnesses. Goals include the following (in order of priority):

- Complete prevention
- Early detection
- Stopping progression

Example The safety committee at an orthotics manufacturer noted that several workers had developed carpal tunnel syndrome. Some were recovering from surgery, and some were still out of work or on modified duty. Most of the injured had worked on a particular process that involved repetitive motion of the wrist. To prevent more cases of carpal tunnel syndrome, the committee redesigned the process so that fewer wrist motions were required, instituted frequent job rotation and hand-exercise breaks, and provided ergonomically redesigned cutting tools. After a general screening for carpal tunnel syndrome, those employees who had early signs or symptoms were reassigned and sent for medical examination and physical therapy. Those who had undergone surgery or had active cases were brought back in permanent positions not involving any repetitive motions of the wrist.

Safety Education

Once the committee has completed its hazard evaluation, it is responsible for recommending topics for safety training programs, identifying those who should attend, and asking for follow-up to see that training has been completed. The committee can also recommend training methods, which may include on- or off-site presentations by outside consultants or in-house experts, films, videos, reading assignments, or other educational approaches.

The committee should ensure that management allows adequate time for safety training during normal working hours. Taking time from production sends a strong message that management considers safety as important as production.

Example An occupational health nurse consultant was asked to give a presentation on bloodborne pathogens to a chemical company's first-aid team on a Saturday morning. Management advised team members that although attendance was "voluntary," anyone not attending would be dropped from the team. Since the normal work week was Monday through Friday, the nurse prevailed on management to reschedule the session on a weekday, which enabled 100% attendance.

Evaluating Effectiveness

One definition of futility is continuing to do the same thing and expecting a different result. Management should require safety committees to monitor their effectiveness *at least annually* by comparing accident statistics with past years' performance and with statistics from similar industries nationally. If there is no improvement, the committee should examine its goals and methods to see whether they are appropriate. It may need to ask for assistance from an outside auditor, such as a safety professional or an insurance loss control specialist.

Safety Incentive Programs

Many employers have instituted programs that reward employees for working safely. The hope is that these programs will increase awareness of safe work practices and decrease false claims and malingering. Although largely anecdotal, reports of effectiveness are enthusiastic.

Critics of safety incentive programs feel that the programs may encourage concealment of injuries that could benefit from early treatment. In addition, they create tremendous peer pressure on anyone taking any time off for a workplace injury or illness, sometimes resulting in an impaired employee inappropriately showing up for work. One employer put a halt to its safety incentive program when co-workers transported a sedated employee from his home to the worksite, carried him up to the front desk to sign in, and then drove him home again.

To set up a safety incentive program, management should write up a summary specifying the desired outcome, the reward, the budget, eligibility, and the valid time period. Rewards can include monthly bonuses, extra days off, reserved parking, trips, gifts, and recognition awards. The number of estimated payoffs multiplied by the value of the reward equals the estimated budget for the time period—typically 1 year.

The desired outcome may be number of days without a lost-time injury or illness. (Some companies exclude repetitive motion disorders, since their onset is thought to occur over many years.) Office workers may not be eligible to participate due to their low claim incidence; however, they should receive recognition or a small bonus. Another desired outcome could be a specific percentage reduction in the number of accidents, with departments competing against other departments for the greatest improvements.

Management should periodically monitor the program to make sure it is being implemented correctly and is not producing unanticipated results, such as under-reporting of injuries and illnesses. At the end of the specified time period, management should evaluate the program's success in achieving established goals. If the safety incentives were successful and well received, the company might want to adjust the goals and rewards for another contest to maintain interest and possibly increase effectiveness.

Example A metal working company was about to be dropped by its insurer due to its high frequency of lost-time injuries, despite an active safety committee, modified-work program, and other controls. The employer instituted a lottery to be held at the end of every month without a lost-time injury. The prize was a gift worth $100 chosen from a catalog containing merchandise. In addition, the employer bought lunch for everyone on the day of the lottery. After beginning this program, the company went 261 calendar days before it had another lost-time accident and reduced its compensation costs proportionately.

Sources of Further Information

Best's Safety Directory, Vols I, II. Oldwick, NJ, A.M. Best, 1994. (Compendium of safety equipment and services by manufacturer/source.)

Colvin RJ. *The Guidebook to Basic Safety Programming.* Chelsea, MI, Lewis, 1992.

Krames Communications, 1100 Grundy Lane, San Bruno, CA 94006-3030; tel. (800) 333-3032. (Wide variety of safety publications, booklets, and videos.)

Lab Safety Supply, Janesville, WI 53547-1368; tel. (800) 356-0783. (Catalog of safety equipment and supplies.)

National Safety Council, 444 N. Michigan Ave., Chicago, IL 60611; tel. (800) 621-7619. (Membership organization with state chapters. Source of safety publications and training courses.)

Occupational Health and Safety. Medical Publications, Inc., 225 N. New Road, Waco, TX 76710; tel. (817) 776-9000. (Monthly safety journal.)

Safe Workplace. National Council on Compensation Insurance, Inc., 750 Park of Commerce Dr., Boca Raton, FL 33487-9951. (Free biannual journal.)

Form 4-1, Safety-Program Report Card

Form 4-2, Safety-Committee Report Card

Purpose of the Forms

- To evaluate adequacy of safety program and committee
- To highlight deficient areas
- To serve as guides for improving safety program and committee

Use of the Forms

- Answer the questions with "yes" or "no."
- Total the "yes" answers at the bottom.
- Read the grade corresponding with the score.
- Take necessary steps to improve the score.

Form 4-1

SAFETY-PROGRAM REPORT CARD

	Y or N
1. Are there regular safety inspections of the workplace and job safety analyses (JSAs)?	
2. Is top management notified of the results of safety inspections and accident statistics, investigations, and recommendations?	
3. Does management provide for continuous improvement of workplace safety through expenditures for facilities, equipment, maintenance, and possibly safety incentives?	
4. Does management budget adequate sums for safety training programs, including purchase of written materials, hiring outside resources, and allowing time off from production duties for staff to attend?	
5. Does management adequately fund the purchase and maintenance of personal protective equipment?	
6. Is there a functioning safety committee?	
7. Do new employees receive job-specific and company-wide safety training prior to assignment?	
8. Does the company have written safety policies and rules that are periodically reviewed and updated?	
9. Is there a formal process in place for disciplining employees who violate safety rules?	
10. Is there a working method for employees to bring safety concerns to the attention of management or the safety committee?	
11. Does management analyze its accident statistics and compare them to those of similar companies?	
12. Is there a designated safety director?	
13. Are outside auditors (insurers, consultants) invited to inspect the premises periodically?	
14. Are employees given performance reviews that include attention to safety?	
15. Is the workplace in full compliance with federal, state, and local worker safety laws, such as OSHA?	
16. Does the company record and report all on-the-job accidents?	

Number of Yes answers = Total Score

GRADE: 14-16=A   12-14=B   10-12=C   8-10=D   Below 8: **Needs improvement!**

Form 4-2

SAFETY-COMMITTEE REPORT CARD

	Y or N
1. Does the committee meet regularly (at least once a month?)	
2. Are there committee members from both management and labor?	
3. Is there an adequate number of committees?	
4. Is there a maximum of 10-15 members?	
5. Is there a written agenda for meetings?	
6. Does the committee record and circulate minutes of its meetings?	
7. Do the meetings start and end on time?	
8. Is there rotating membership on the committee?	
9. Does the committee have management support?	
10. Does the committee have both responsibility and authority?	
11. Does the committee investigate accidents and incidents?	
12. Does it make written recommendations for accident prevention and follow them up?	
13. Does the committee track accident statistics?	
14. Have the frequency and severity of accidents declined in the past 2 years?	
15. Does the committee plan safety programs based on documented needs?	
16. Does the committee evaluate the effectiveness of its safety programs?	

Number of Yes answers = Total Score

GRADE: 14-16=A   12-14=B   10-12=C   8-10=D   Below 8: **Needs improvement!**

5

Hazard Evaluation

The Industrial Revolution brought with it many safety hazards that did not exist in the previous agrarian society. Because of a series of widely publicized industrial accidents and tragedies (such as cancer deaths from occupational asbestos exposure) and pressure from organized labor, in 1970 the federal government (U.S. Department of Labor, Occupational Safety and Health Administration [OSHA]) legislated that each employer has a duty to provide "employment and a place of employment which are free from recognized hazards that are causing or are likely to cause death or serious physical harm to his employees."[1] (OSHA refers to this as the "general duty clause" when it cites an employer for a safety hazard that is not specifically covered by its regulations.)

However, employees continue to be injured on the job by working in unsafe environments. Unsafe conditions are among the easier accident causes to identify and remedy. A good beginning for any safety program is to analyze the worksite for readily apparent hazards.

Example A surgical instrument manufacturer looked over its on-the-job accidents for the previous 2 years and found that many injuries were occurring among its field salespeople, who hurt their backs when hefting 40-lb bags of instruments in and out of vehicles. The safety committee found problems in work flow. It recommended eliminating an unsafe condition by redistributing the samples into two smaller bags or using wheeled carriers.

---

1 USC §654 (a) (1).

Initial Hazard Survey

The safety committee should conduct an initial hazard survey. If it feels overwhelmed by the task or lacks confidence in its abilities, it can request assistance from outside specialists.

Available Professional Assistance

To draw upon outside resources, ask your workers' comp insurance carrier to send someone from its loss-control department to assist the safety committee. These consultants can provide valuable guidance at no charge.

You may also request on-site technical assistance through OSHA's Consultation Program (see Appendix B), which is delivered through state governmental agencies. This program is a good source to obtain industrial hygiene, safety, and occupational health advisory services. However, these OSHA-funded consultants do require participants to correct any "imminent danger" condition immediately or be reported to OSHA's enforcement branch. Call your local or regional OSHA office if you need further information about hazard surveys and advisory services (see Appendix C).

Some registered nurses have advanced education and experience and provide consulting in workplace safety and health, regulatory compliance programs, and training. Contact the American Association of Occupational Health Nurses (AAOHN) for a list of nurse consultants or the American Board for Occupational Health Nurses for a list of certified occupational health nurses (COHNs) in your state (see "Sources of Further Information").

Practical tip A local occupational health clinic may provide walk-through hazard surveys at no charge, in exchange for referring employees needing health services, such as pre-placement testing, audiometric screening, or post-injury care, to the clinic.

Procedure for Conducting a Safety Survey

The safety committee should divide the company up into locations or departments, such as Main Office, Shipping, Spray Booth, or Outside Sales. The committee should then conduct walk-throughs, using the **Hazard Checklist** (Form 5-1) as a guide.

Practical tip Ask employees in each department what they view as safety hazards. The safety committee is visiting only briefly, whereas regular employees have more extensive knowledge of perceived dangers and concerns. In addition, involving employees in the survey will improve compliance with needed improvements.

Once the committee has identified hazards, it should plan ways to eliminate them. Chapter 6 explains this process in greater detail. Often, a hazard is caused by human behavior that has a complex solution requiring careful study and analysis.

Example The safety committee noted that a guard had been removed from a high-speed chopping machine. It added "guard verification" to the supervisor's weekly inspection checklist. The guard was found removed on several occasions and was re-attached. After several reports of this, the committee investigated and found that night-shift workers were removing guards to boost production rates. The committee notified higher management, which warned the employees that any further guard removals would result in dismissal of the responsible person or persons. The committee then requested that management review its productivity bonus system, which was driving workers to take safety risks.

Safety Self-Inspections

Once the safety committee has completed an initial safety survey using the Hazard Checklist, it should request that each department conduct regular inspections of specific areas or processes to keep potential hazards under control and to ensure that safety equipment and programs are maintained. For example, the safety committee may have noted on the Hazard Checklist that the cleanliness of break areas needs improvement. It might assign to the housekeeping department a weekly inspection of these areas for cleanliness and ask for monthly summary reports.

The **Inspection Report** (Form 5-2) can be used for departments' regular inspections. A sample completed form is shown below:

Inspection Report

Area to be Inspected <u>Machinery in Winding</u>

Frequency: __✔__ Weekly

Department:	Inspector:	Date:
Winding	M. Mills	10/06/93
Expectations:	**Findings:**	**Recommendations**
1. All machines guarded 2. Maintenance current 3. Lockout documented 4. Oil cleaned up	1. Guards removed from 2 of 6	1. Supervisor to reinforce training.

The safety committee should make it clear that supervisors, not committee members, are responsible for maintaining a safe work environment. The committee should act as an overseer of the routine inspection process, without being directly responsible for identifying and correcting safety problems.

Sources of Further Information

American Association of Occupational Health Nurses, 50 Lenox Pointe, Atlanta, GA 30324-3176; tel. (404) 262-1162. (List of occupational health nurse consultants.)

American Board for Occupational Health Nurses, 10503 North Cedarburg Road, Mequon, WI 53092-4403; tel. (414)242-0704. (List of certified occupational health nurses [COHNs] by state.)

Colvin RJ. *The Guidebook to Basic Safety Programming.* Chelsea, MI, Lewis, 1992.

Peterson D. *Safety Management: A Human Approach* (2nd ed). Goshen, NY, Aloray, 1988.

U.S. Department of Labor, Occupational Safety and Health Administration. *OSHA Handbook for Small Businesses.* Washington, DC, U.S. Government Printing Office, 1992.

Form 5-1, Hazard Checklist

Purpose of the Form

- To outline annual or semiannual hazard survey
- To document specific deficiencies needing correction
- To provide benchmarks for subsequent inspections
- To plan for needed improvements

Use of the Form

- The safety committee should use a different checklist for each area inspected.
- Add items as needed to the checklist.
- The safety committee should list each item needing improvement and prepare a plan to abate hazards.

Form 5 - 1

HAZARD CHECKLIST*

DEPARTMENT _____ DATE _____

WORK FLOW
OK Improve

☐ ☐ Work flow process efficient; no unnecessary motion required
☐ ☐ Equipment for materials handling (fork trucks, conveyors, hand trucks, cranes, hoists, pulleys) safe
☐ ☐ Heights ergonomically correct for processing work (bench, desk, chair, shelves)
☐ ☐ Floor loads adequate for weight of work; floor loading signs present
☐ ☐ No projection of materials into traffic areas
☐ ☐ Materials storage adequate, safe
☐ ☐ Materials-handling methods, including frequency and amounts of loads lifted, within acceptable limits

☐ ☐

BUILDING AND GROUNDS
OK Improve

☐ ☐ Floors, walls, ceilings structurally sound
☐ ☐ Exits marked and kept clear and unlocked
☐ ☐ Doors open and close freely
☐ ☐ Stairs: non-slip surface, handrails present, riser/tread ratios meet OSHA standards
☐ ☐ Walkways and aisles clear; non-slip footing
☐ ☐ Ramps clear
☐ ☐ Platforms structurally sound
☐ ☐ Driveways clear of foot traffic
☐ ☐ Parking lot free of snow, ice, water, broken pavement, and other hazards
☐ ☐

SANITATION
OK Improve

☐ ☐ Cleanliness of break areas, toilets, wash facilities, cafeterias, food storage and handling areas
☐ ☐ Drinking water potable
☐ ☐ Garbage and waste disposal adequate and frequent
☐ ☐

HOUSEKEEPING PROGRAM
OK Improve

☐ ☐ Waste-disposal area free of litter
☐ ☐ Maintenance program for tools
☐ ☐ Safe material storage (fire or explosion hazards)
☐ ☐ Procedure for leak-and-spill control in place
☐ ☐ Cleaning methods and schedules adequate for hazards (biological, chemical, electrical)
☐ ☐

Workers' Comp Management from A to Z: A "How to" Guide with Forms. © Nancy Nivison Menzel, OEM Press, Beverly, MA, 1994.

ELECTRICITY

OK Improve
☐   ☐   Cords not in travel paths
☐   ☐   Lockout-tagout program in effect
☐   ☐   Written electrical safety program, including training
☐   ☐

LIGHTING

OK Improve
☐   ☐   Type and intensity appropriate for type of work
☐   ☐   Diffusion provided where needed
☐   ☐   Glare and shadow control
☐   ☐   If UV light exposure (including direct sun), eye and skin protection provided
☐   ☐

HEATING AND VENTILATION

OK Improve
☐   ☐   Temperature correct for working environment (avoid temperature extremes)
☐   ☐   Adequate natural and artificial ventilation
☐   ☐   Adequate exhaust for exposures, including chemical hoods
☐   ☐

MACHINERY

OK Improve
☐   ☐   Flywheels; gears; shafts; pulleys; belts; couplings; sprockets; chains; frames; controls; brakes guarded if necessary and in good working order
☐   ☐   Hazard-free materials feeding
☐   ☐   Maintenance scheduled and completed
☐   ☐   Use of grounding
☐   ☐   Lockout/tagout program in place
☐   ☐   Work space adequate
☐   ☐   Guards in place where needed
☐   ☐   Emergency stops functional
☐   ☐   Metallic fumes, dusts, and oil mists controlled
☐   ☐   Job-safety analyses conducted
☐   ☐   Sharp edges padded or guarded
☐   ☐

PERSONNEL

OK Improve
☐   ☐   Training given in machine operation, work practices, methods of cleaning or adjusting machinery
☐   ☐   Appropriate clothing worn
☐   ☐   Personal protective equipment (ear protection, respirators, safety glasses, shoes)
☐   ☐   Use of guards
☐   ☐   Appropriate behavior (following safety rules)
☐   ☐

Workers' Comp Management from A to Z: A "How to" Guide with Forms. © Nancy Nivison Menzel, OEM Press, Beverly, MA, 1994.

Form 5-1, page 2

NOISE

OK	Improve	
☐	☐	Sound-level measurements done if noisy environment
☐	☐	Hearing conservation program in place in any area with noise over 85 dB
☐	☐	

HAND AND POWER TOOLS

OK	Improve	
☐	☐	Purchasing standards established
☐	☐	Periodic inspection
☐	☐	Proper storage and repair
☐	☐	Maintenance program established
☐	☐	Grounding used
☐	☐	Vibration controlled
☐	☐	

SECURITY

OK	Improve	
☐	☐	Parking lot well lit and patrolled
☐	☐	Access to premises well lit and secure
☐	☐	Warning alarms or other notification system available
☐	☐	Security personnel on staff
☐	☐	

EMERGENCY EQUIPMENT

OK	Improve	
☐	☐	Generators, fire pumps, alarms present and operative
☐	☐	

CHEMICALS

OK	Improve	
☐	☐	Hazardous potentials known
☐	☐	Required instrumental monitoring (OSHA-regulated substances) carried out
☐	☐	Safe storage, handling, transportation
☐	☐	Spill-control plan in place
☐	☐	Lawful disposal program followed
☐	☐	Warning signs present
☐	☐	Hazard Communication program up to date
☐	☐	Protective clothing and equipment in use
☐	☐	MSDSs and chemical inventory up to date
☐	☐	Tracking of starting, intermediate, final, and waste stream materials
☐	☐	

Workers' Comp Management from A to Z: A "How to" Guide with Forms. © Nancy Nivison Menzel, OEM Press, Beverly, MA, 1994.

Form 5-1, page 3

FIRE PREVENTION

OK Improve

☐ ☐ Extinguishers, alarms, sprinklers present and inspected
☐ ☐ Smoking rules enforced
☐ ☐ Emergency exits marked and clear
☐ ☐ Segregation of reactive materials
☐ ☐ NFPA-designated operations
☐ ☐ Explosion-proof fixtures in hazardous locations
☐ ☐ Waste disposed promptly
☐ ☐ Written fire plan
☐ ☐ Periodic fire drills
☐ ☐

MAINTENANCE

OK Improve

☐ ☐ Regularly scheduled, completed, and recorded
☐ ☐ Effectiveness adequate
☐ ☐ Materials and equipment used appropriate
☐ ☐ Responsibility for maintenance of personal protective equipment established
☐ ☐

HAZARDOUS WASTE

OK Improve

☐ ☐ Exposure prevented
☐ ☐ Safe storage, with required labeling
☐ ☐ Disposal tracked
☐ ☐

ERGONOMICS

OK Improve

☐ ☐ Person/machine/task/equipment interfaces correct for size and physical abilities of employees
☐ ☐ Proper lifting postures and load sizes
☐ ☐ Mechanical assistance available for lifting, pushing, pulling, carrying
☐ ☐

REPETITIVE MOTION EXPOSURES

OK Improve

☐ ☐ Few repetitions or movement of extremities, little use of force, no awkward postures
☐ ☐

WELDING

OK Improve

☐ ☐ Adequate protection: personal protective equipment, safe location, welding policies in place, fuel cylinders transported on chained carriers, stored in fire/explosion-proof/secure areas
☐ ☐

Workers' Comp Management from A to Z: A "How to" Guide with Forms. © Nancy Nivison Menzel, OEM Press, Beverly, MA, 1994.

DISASTER/EMERGENCY PLANNING
OK Improve
☐ ☐ Drills conducted
☐ ☐ Written plan covering many types of disaster
☐ ☐ Disaster team in place
☐ ☐

MEDICAL SERVICES AND FIRST AID
OK Improve
☐ ☐ Emergency numbers posted
☐ ☐ MSDSs available
☐ ☐ Trained first-aid team on site or medical clinic immediately nearby
☐ ☐ If first-aid team on site, then bloodborne pathogens protection program in effect
☐ ☐

RECORDKEEPING AND SIGNAGE
OK Improve
☐ ☐ OSHA Notice posted
☐ ☐ OSHA 200 log current and posted annually
☐ ☐ Other safety notices, if any, posted
☐ ☐

MISCELLANEOUS
OK Improve
☐ ☐ Outside contractor notification procedure followed
☐ ☐ PIV (forktruck safety) in place
☐ ☐ Overhead-crane safety program
☐ ☐ Ionizing/non-ionizing radiation controlled
☐ ☐ Biological exposures identified and controlled
☐ ☐ Commercial driver's license program in place
☐ ☐ Confined-space program in place
☐ ☐ Overall OSHA compliance
☐ ☐ Body fluid exposures identified and controlled
☐ ☐

OTHER
OK Improve
☐ ☐
☐ ☐
☐ ☐
☐ ☐
☐ ☐
☐ ☐
☐ ☐
☐ ☐
☐ ☐

*Adapted from information on self-inspection in: U.S. Department of Labor, Occupational Safety and Health Administration. *OSHA Handbook for Small Businesses*. Washington, DC, U.S. Government Printing Office, 1992. Pp 19 - 36.

Workers' Comp Management from A to Z: A "How to" Guide with Forms. © Nancy Nivison Menzel, OEM Press, Beverly, MA, 1994.

Form 5-1, page 5

Form 5-2, Inspection Report

The Inspection Report documents the date and findings of the inspection. If corrected hazards keep recurring, the committee should find out whether there has been a failure of management or an ineffective solution for abating the hazard.

Purpose of the Form

- To assign regular inspection times and responsibilities to the appropriate departments or individuals
- To maintain safe conditions
- To identify problems
- To identify recurrent problems

Use of the Form

- Sort inspection tasks by area and frequency (e.g., fire extinguishers and exits weekly; MSDSs monthly).
- Name the person responsible for the inspection.
- List expectations for conditions of area inspected.
- Note any abnormal conditions and correction suggestions.
- Forward to the safety committee any reports showing deficiencies.

Form 5 - 2

INSPECTION REPORT

Areas to be inspected _____

Frequency: _____ Monthly _____ Weekly _____ Daily _____ Yearly _____ Other ( )

Department		Inspector		Date
Expectations		Findings		Recommendations

Workers' Comp Management from A to Z: A "How to" Guide with Forms. © Nancy Nivison Menzel, OEM Press, Beverly, MA, 1994.

6

Establishing a Strategic Hazard-Control Program

Once the safety committee has completed its risk assessment of the workplace, it should devise a plan to control identified hazards or deficiencies.

Focus of Program

This strategic plan should be based on the relative severity of the identified hazard and the probability of it causing injuries or illnesses. Initially, the committee should not consider the cost or time involved to abate the hazards. The major focus should be on the potential for harm. Form 6-1, **Strategic Hazard-Control Plan**, is intended for use in formulating the plan.

Establishing Target Dates for Program Implementation

The next step is to establish target dates for completion using available resources. If the risk seems high, but the period to eliminate it seems prolonged, the safety committee should present the situation to management to enlist help.

> **Example** A safety survey of a construction company identified pneumatic jackhammers that exceeded safe noise levels and transmitted high amounts of vibration. One of the employees had early signs of vibration damage to his hands (vibration white-finger syndrome). None of the division managers had budgeted any money to buy newer vibration-attenuated jackhammers; the next budget cycle was nearly a year away. Because the hazard was already causing injury, the committee approached the company manager and requested assistance. The

manager immediately bought new jackhammers with funds from another account, eliminating vibration, excessive noise, and the need for hearing protection.

Taking Specific Steps for Hazard Abatement

Finally, once the committee has established realistic dates for hazard abatement, it must come up with specific steps and a timetable for completion, including assigning responsibility (see Form 6-2, **Play-by-Play Hazard-Control Plan**). The safety committee should oversee the project by periodically reviewing progress and providing assistance when needed.

Sources of Further Information

Occupational Hazards: The Magazine of Safety, Health and Environmental Management. Penton Publishing, 1100 Superior Avenue, Cleveland, OH 44114-2543.

Kase DW, Wiese KJ. *Safety Auditing: A Management Tool.* New York, Van Nostrand Reinhold, 1990.

Form 6-1, Strategic Hazard-Control Plan

Purpose of the Form

- To rank hazards by degree of risk
- To focus attention and resources on identified problems
- To initiate the process of hazard abatement

Use of the Form

- List all identified hazards or deficiencies (e.g., "No written disaster plan") under the "Opponents" section.
- Once all hazards are listed, assign a rank, starting with 1 for the most serious, just as a coach might rank opponents.
- Estimate a date for "victory" over the hazard.
- Refer to these dates periodically to check progress; record final dates of completion.

Form 6-1

STRATEGIC HAZARD-CONTROL PLAN

Ranking	Opponents	Targeted Victory Date	Actual Victory Date

Workers' Comp Management from A to Z: A "How to" Guide with Forms. © Nancy Nivison Menzel, OEM Press, Beverly, MA, 1994.

Form 6-2, Play-by-Play Hazard-Control Plan

Purpose of the Form

- To identify the person responsible for hazard abatement
- To describe the specific steps needed to accomplish the goal
- To evaluate progress toward achieving goal

Use of the Form

- List the hazard or deficiency and its ranking after "Opponent."
- Identify the employee responsible for abatement next to "Captain."
- Either the captain or the safety committee should further break down the task into the specific steps needed to achieve results, along with the employee "Player" assigned to complete them, as shown below:

Opponent (Hazard): No written disaster plan. **Ranking:** 3 **Captain:** Ann Wilson

Specific Steps	Player Assigned	Scheduled	Completed
Form task force to write plan	A. Wilson	04/10/94	
Write plan	Task force	05/10/94	
Have safety committee and management review and approve plan	Task force	06/10/94	

- Use the form to review progress toward completion dates.

Form 6-2

PLAY-BY-PLAY HAZARD-CONTROL PLAN

Opponent(Hazard): _____   Ranking: _____   Captain: _____

Specific Steps	Player Assigned	Scheduled	Completed

Workers' Comp Management from A to Z: A "How to" Guide with Forms. © Nancy Nivison Menzel, OEM Press, Beverly, MA, 1994.

7

Establishing Health and Safety Policies

Formulating Written Health and Safety Policies

As a first step, any company that is serious about safety should formulate a written policy that makes its intentions clear to employees (see Form 7-1, **Health and Safety Policy**). Think of it as a mission statement, a corporate pledge, a guiding philosophy, from which all other parts of the safety program flow. A written health and safety policy acts as a guide to action and influences all employees from the top down. It should incorporate safety as part of the continuous quality-improvement process.

The chief executive officer (CEO) should issue the safety policy, to further emphasize that the company values the protection of its employees. In addition, management support of safety translates into better public perception of the company's product.

> **Example** A group from a prospective client company toured a building-materials manufacturer, which was promoting the superior quality of its products. There were broken pieces of the material scattered along the plant walkways and pieces crushed by forklifts in the parking area. The employee-break areas were covered by dust from the manufacturing process. Unpleasant chemical odors filled the air. The perception was that of a facility with little regard for its employees' safety. This negative perception clouded the group's assessment, and after the tour, all the advertising rhetoric in the world couldn't convince the prospective client of the product's supposed superior quality.

The statement should describe specific responsibilities for management, supervisors, and employees. The policy should outline the basics of the safety program as well.

All new employees should be asked to read the policy statement prior to beginning work. In addition, a copy of the policy should be posted prominently in each work area.

Setting Standards for Safe Behavior

Companies should also construct a list that emphasizes what behaviors are expected or prohibited (see Form 7-2, **Employee Safety Behaviors**). They can ask employees to read and sign the safe-behavior list prior to employment. The signed list can later serve as a basis for taking disciplinary action, if needed.

The time to take disciplinary action is prior to misbehavior that may cause an accident. In some states, an employee's "serious and willful misconduct" may be grounds for denying compensation, but intention is difficult to prove. It is better to prevent the accident than to try to prove fault in an essentially no-fault system.

Example The night manager of a supermarket observed a teenage employee riding on the conveyor belt that carried cardboard cartons of materials from the basement storage area to the sales floor. The manager warned the employee to stop riding the belt, since it was not designed to carry humans and consequently did not have guards at its mid-point. The manager caught the youth twice more, each time advising him that he was not to do it again.

One night, when the employee hopped on the conveyor, his shoelaces got caught in an unguarded gear. He was unable to remove his shoe and suffered a traumatic amputation of the right foot. The injury was fully compensable under workers' compensation, since it was viewed as an accident arising out of, and in the course of, employment. The fact that the employee had disobeyed safety rules was not considered.

After the first infraction, the manager should have given a written warning to the employee that further violations would be grounds for termination. If the employee had been found riding the conveyor after that, the manager should have fired him. Then the employee would still have his foot, and the employer's workers' comp premium would not have escalated.

Sources of Further Information

Contact your insurance carrier's loss-control department for copies of recommended health and safety policies.

Network with other organizations in similar industries to exchange health and safety policies.

Ask trade organizations or business associations for copies of their standard safety and health policies.

Form 7-1, Health and Safety Policy

Purpose of the Form

- To put the company's leadership pledge for maintaining a safe workplace in writing
- To advise employees of management's commitment
- To outline elements of the safety program
- To alert employees to their safety responsibilities

Use of the Form

- The chief executive officer (CEO) should revise the policy as desired.
- Type the policy on company letterhead, to be signed by the CEO.
- Post the policy in a prominent place in all work areas.
- Have new employees read the policy prior to job assignment.

Workers' Comp Management from A to Z

HEALTH AND SAFETY POLICY*

We are committed to protecting the personal health and safety of each of our employees. We accomplish this by means of a safety program that is designed to eliminate injuries and illnesses through a process of continuous improvement. Accidents are unnecessary and preventable and have no role in our efforts to improve quality in all our operations.

Our health and safety program includes:

- Regular inspections to find and eliminate unsafe conditions or practices, to control health hazards, and to comply with all regulations

- Substituting less hazardous materials or processes when feasible

- Administrative measures, such as job reassignment

- Mechanical and physical safeguards

- Engineering controls

- Providing personal protective equipment when the hazard cannot be abated by other means

- Safety and health rules that regulate the behavior of all employees as a condition of employment

- Prompt investigation of every accident to prevent similar accidents from occurring in the future

- Timely, professional medical care for all injuries or illnesses

- Recognition and awards for outstanding safety service or performance

- Analysis of accident statistics

Everyone who works here shares responsibility for safety. Achieving a safe work environment requires *cooperation* between management and employees:

- The employer provides the leadership and resources needed to ensure safe conditions and work practices.

Workers' Comp Management from A to Z: A "How to" Guide with Forms. © Nancy Nivison Menzel, OEM Press, Beverly, MA, 1994.

- Supervisors carry out the safety program by making sure that all operations are performed with the highest regard for everyone's safety and health. They shall praise safe work practices and reeducate employees working in an unsafe manner.

- If supervisors discover any unsafe condition, they shall take corrective action as soon as possible. If any employee is in imminent danger of harm, the responsible supervisor shall stop the hazardous operation until the hazard is eliminated.

- Employees cooperate and participate in all aspects of the safety program, including complying with rules, reporting safety concerns or hazards, notifying co-workers about unsafe work practices, and continuously practicing safety while performing their duties.

Safe work practices are a part of every employee's performance evaluation. Working together, we can create a safe and productive environment to accomplish our goals.

_____   _____
Signature and title   Date

*   Adapted from information on health and safety policy statements in: U.S. Department of Labor, Occupational Safety and Health Administration. *OSHA Handbook for Small Businesses*. Washington, DC, U.S. Government Printing Office, 1992. Pp 50-52.

Form 7-2, Employee Safety Behaviors

Purpose of the Form

- To notify employees of company's expectations for behavior on the job
- To serve as basis for future disciplinary action, if needed

Use of the Form

- The safety committee or CEO should revise the code as desired.
- New employees should be asked to read and sign the form prior to job assignment.
- A signed copy should be kept in the employee's personnel folder.

Form 7-2

EMPLOYEE SAFETY BEHAVIORS*

1. All employees shall conduct themselves in a safe manner and have a duty to report all unsafe conditions or unsafe work practices to their supervisors.

2. Supervisors are responsible for employee compliance with safety regulations and shall discipline employees who disregard the rules.

3. Management shall educate employees in accident prevention through frequent emergency drills, training sessions, and educational materials about workplace safety and health.

4. Anyone under the influence of alcohol or drugs shall not be allowed on the job while impaired. Supervisors shall refer employees who abuse alcohol or drugs to the Employee Assistance Program.

5. Employees whose ability or alertness is impaired by fatigue, illness, or other causes shall not be allowed on the job until they no longer pose a danger to themselves or their co-workers.

6. Employees required to wear personal protective equipment shall comply and keep it in good working order.

7. Horseplay, teasing, harassment, and similar inappropriate behavior on the job is prohibited.

8. Before working with or handling heavy materials or equipment, employees shall plan work carefully to prevent injuries. For example, when lifting objects over 40 lb, employees should seek assistance from co-workers, use mechanical devices as hoists, or defer lifting until they devise a safe method to accomplish the task. For lifting objects less than 40 lb, employees should bend their knees and use the large muscles of the legs instead of the smaller muscles of the back.

I have read and will follow these employee safety behaviors.

_____   _____
Employee signature   Date

* Adapted from information on health and safety policy statements in: U.S. Department of Labor, Occupational Safety and Health Administration. *OSHA Handbook for Small Businesses*. Washington, DC, U.S. Government Printing Office, 1992. Pp 50-52.

8

Establishing Injured Worker Policies

Employees are human and subject to injuries and illnesses that limit their work abilities on a scale from partial to complete, from temporary to permanent. Unlike broken machinery, it is costly and unproductive to toss aside employees who can no longer perform their original work assignments due to injury or illness. Since the passage of the Americans with Disabilities Act (ADA), it may even be illegal to do so.

Prior to the advent of skyrocketing workers' comp premiums, it was common for managers to mentally "write off" injured employees unless and until they were ready to fully return to work, particularly if they had caused problems in the past. Many supervisors had the attitude that the employee had now become the insurance company's responsibility (and headache). With few or no consequences for having this "out-of-sight, out-of-mind" attitude, supervisors brought in replacement workers or did without.

Realities Regarding Work-Related Injuries and Illnesses

Suddenly faced with huge workers' comp premiums, companies began to look for ways to reduce costs. Since *indemnity* (wage replacement) costs make up more than half of most workers' comp claim expenses, the length of time an injured worker is out has a profound effect on the severity (cost) of the claim. It became obvious that one way to reduce the cost of claims was to try to reduce indemnity payments.

Some states have tried to lower indemnity payments through legislative means by reducing the percentage of wage replacement allowed, by denying further increases, or by limiting the length of time such payments may be made. Savvy employers have responded by bringing injured workers back to work as soon as medically feasible, thereby terminating or lowering the indemnity payments.

It soon became obvious that injured workers who were brought back to work in *any* capacity during rehabilitation recovered at a faster rate than those who were completely separated from work and presumably resting at home. This is not unlike the revolution in postoperative care, when the experience in military field hospitals disrupted the conventional logic of keeping surgical patients in bed for weeks. As soldiers were mobilized immediately after surgery, the surgeons noted a dramatic decrease in complications like blood clots. As a result, modern postoperative care dictates early ambulation for almost all patients.

Benefits of Early Return to Work

Earlier return to work promotes reconnection with the workplace and co-workers. In addition, the work habit is less disrupted. Just as those returning from a vacation find the first few days difficult, so too do those returning to work after long absences due to injury or illness. Even a modified-duty assignment of a few hours' work a day keeps intact the habits of rising, personal grooming, travel, mental acuity, and physical fitness.

Absence Makes the Claim Grow Longer

Prolonged absences promote work *deconditioning*. There is a workers' comp maxim: "The longer you're out, the longer you're out." The likelihood of an injured employee's permanently returning to work is inversely proportional to the length of the absence. After a 6-month disability absence, for example, the odds are slim that the employee will ever return. At this point, the injured employee's "job" has become fighting the insurer, the employer, and the system. The injured employee forges a bond with his or her attorney, a bond that displaces the connection with former co-workers.

Other Effects of Absence

Disconnection from normal routines and familiar co-workers, anxiety over impaired physical abilities, and economic insecurity combine to promote depression in those hurt on the job or with work-related illnesses. Depression heightens the perception of pain, and vice versa—increased pain can worsen depression. The injured, increasingly anxious, and isolated employee stays at home, watching daytime television shows that are peppered with appealing lawyer advertisements: "Injured at work? Don't be cheated out of what is owed to you! Call us—we care!"

For all these reasons, it makes sense for employers to do everything possible to encourage an early return to work. Even if the employee is temporarily not performing the same job at the previous productivity rate, the employee's efforts can make a useful contribution elsewhere in the organization.

Appointing a Workers' Comp Coordinator

Managing an early-return-to-work program requires coordination of information among, and negotiation with, the treating medical professional, the supervisor, the human resource department, the insurance adjuster, and the injured employee. Companies that have been successful with modified-duty programs often have appointed a workers' comp coordinator (WCC) to help direct the events that profoundly influence the outcome of the case and thus the cost to the employer.

The WCC should be an employee of the company or someone specifically contracted by the company to manage its cases, such as a disability or rehabilitation case-management firm. Organizations with 500 or more employees should employ a registered nurse as the workers' comp coordinator. Employees trust nurses and look to them for guidance when injured or ill. Nurses also help maintain employee wellness, prevent injuries and illnesses, and control the cost of general medical care. Contact the American Board for Occupational Health Nurses or the American Association of Occupational Health Nurses (see "Sources of Further Information").

If no nurse is present, case coordination can be done by someone with an interest in the project and a caring attitude. Although extremely helpful, medical knowledge is not required. A medical dictionary and close questioning of medical providers will help WCCs understand common diagnoses, treatment, and physical limitations. The responsibility for case coordination is often delegated to the human resources or the medical department, which should designate one person as the main WCC.

Instituting a Modified-Duty Policy and Program

Before a company institutes a modified-duty program, it should establish a policy with clear guidelines, so that it is applied fairly and employees understand from the beginning that encouraging early return to work is routine and not an action intended to single them out. (See Form 8-1, **Company Policy on Modified-Duty Assignments.**)

The policy should emphasize that these assignments are temporary, time-limited, and transitional steps in recovery. Asking the employee to sign a written description of a specific modified-duty assignment helps to emphasize this.

Example A nurse with a back injury was prohibited from all lifting. The hospital reassigned her from the orthopedics unit to the education department on a month-to-month basis. When her lifting abilities began to be restored, the nurse refused to return to her former unit, arguing that the hospital had "transferred" her. The hospital reviewed documentation, signed by the nurse, that the reassignment was a transitional assignment and not a transfer. The nurse returned to the orthopedics unit.

If the employees are unionized, make sure that the union participates in drafting the modified-duty policy and that its adoption does not violate any collective bargaining agreements.

Example A utility company encountered strong union resistance to a proposed change in the collective bargaining agreement that would have allowed injured or ill workers to be reassigned to "lighter" tasks while they recovered. Concurrent with this dispute, a well-liked employee who was hurt off the job used up all his sick time, so union members were donating their sick days to keep his paychecks coming. After several weeks of this generous activity, the union asked management to make an exception to the "no light duty" rule and allow this particular employee to work in a modified capacity. However, management held firm until the union relented and agreed to allow "light duty" for all injured or ill employees.

If the company is unable to bring certain injured employees back to modified duty due to either the severity of the injury or lack of appropriate work, the company should place the employee on a *leave of absence* for a specified period of time, typically until the next medical exam. The leave should be extended until the employee has reached maximum medical improvement and a final decision has been made about whether the employee can return to work.

Effect of Other Legislation

Americans with Disabilities Act

The Americans with Disabilities Act (ADA) of 1990 is a far-reaching law designed to eliminate discrimination against individuals with disabilities. As such, the law impinges on workers' comp. Policies prohibiting the return of workers until they have recovered 100% may be in violation of the ADA if the injured employee is capable of performing the essential functions of the job. However, employers who have developed and implemented a reasonable program for returning injured employees to the job are building a strong defense against any ADA claims.

Family and Medical Leave Act

The Family and Medical Leave Act of 1993 may apply to workers' comp cases, enabling those hurt on the job to take up to 12 weeks off with the same or similar job available for them upon their return, among many other benefits. Before establishing a policy governing the handling of employees who are out of work due to an on-the-job injury, employers should have it reviewed by an attorney familiar with federal and state employment and workers' compensation laws.

Establishing Employee-Supportive Personnel Policies

Employers should consider that some workers' comp claims may result from job stress and dissatisfaction as well as personal problems and pressures. Employers who routinely require employees to work over 40 hours must accept that they have increased the exposure of these employees to all workplace hazards, particularly repetitive motion disorders, with predictable results.

Some workers' comp claims could be prevented by reviewing personnel policies and revising them to take into consideration the need for rest and the reality that employees have many responsibilities outside of work. Examples of supportive policies and programs include:

- Flexible hours, job sharing, child or elder care
- Adequate paid vacation and holiday time
- Reasonable working hours, with limits on mandatory overtime
- Encouragement of exercise programs
- Employee Assistance Program
- On-site wellness programs, including stress management
- Healthy food available for on-site meals

Sources of Further Information

American Association of Occupational Health Nurses, 50 Lenox Pointe, Atlanta, GA 30324-3176; tel. (404) 262-1162. (Information about employing an occupational health nurse.)

American Board for Occupational Health Nurses, 10503 North Cedarburg Road, Mequon, WI 53092-4403; tel. (414)242-0704. (List of certified occupational health nurses [COHNs] by state.)

Dent GL. *Return to Work ... By Design.* Stockton, CA, Martin-Dennison, 1990.

Stedman's Medical Dictionary (25th ed). Baltimore, MD, Williams & Wilkins, 1990.

Form 8-1, Company Policy on Modified-Duty Assignments

Purpose of the Form

- To explain to employees the company's philosophy about early return to work
- To clarify responsibilities in the modified-duty process

Use of the Form

- Review the policy during orientation of new employees.
- Review the effectiveness of the policy annually (i.e., severity statistics).

Form 8-1

COMPANY POLICY ON MODIFIED-DUTY ASSIGNMENTS

Each of our employees makes a valuable contribution to our company, where we strive to provide a safe work environment. Despite our best efforts, if a work-related injury or illness does occur, we make an effort to ensure that employees will receive expert medical care in a timely manner.

To assist in rehabilitation following an accident, our company offers injured or ill employees modified-duty assignments based on their current abilities. Returning to work in a modified capacity helps to promote full recovery. These assignments are transitional and are reviewed every 30 days. If the company is unable to accommodate the employee's work restrictions or if the employee has been ordered not to work in any capacity, the employee will be placed on a leave of absence with periodic review of work ability. All leaves of absence are in compliance with the Family and Medical Leave Act.

==

SCOPE

[All facilities]

==

PROCEDURE FOR ASSIGNMENTS

1. The workers' compensation coordinator (WCC) will obtain an assessment of the injured employee's current work capabilities from the treating medical professional prior to approving any return to work.

2. The WCC will notify the employee's supervisor when an employee has been cleared to return to work in either a full or transitional capacity. The WCC will specify in writing the type, nature, and duration of any restrictions. It is the supervisor's responsibility to locate a suitable job within the department that will make use of the employee's abilities without exceeding restrictions.

3. The supervisor will accommodate restrictions by creating a temporary transitional work assignment that may:

    a. eliminate or modify tasks or equipment in current job

    b. reduce work hours to accommodate endurance abilities or treatment schedule, or

    c. include suitable duties from other positions.

4. The transitional job's title is "Modified-Duty Assignment." The supervisor will not make any assignment that exceeds the employee's work capabilities. The supervisor will give the WCC and the injured employee a written description of this temporary assignment's duties, hours, and responsibilities prior to the start of work.

5. If the supervisor is unable to modify a job, schedule, or position to accommodate an injured employee who is ready to return to work, the WCC will refer the employee to the department head, who will be responsible for relocating the employee in another area or department that can offer a suitable assignment. If the department head is unable to locate a suitable assignment, the WCC will search for an appropriate placement.

6. The originating department will continue to be responsible for the injured employee, regardless of any temporary assignment.

7. If the company cannot place the employee in a modified-duty assignment or if the employee is unable to work at all, the company will place the employee on a leave of absence until the next medical examination or until a final decision on work status has been reached.

8. Any changes in modified-duty assignments must be approved by the WCC.

9. Any employee returning to a modified-duty assignment will continue to receive the pre-injury rate of pay.

10. The WCC will review each modified-duty assignment or leave of absence and obtain an update on current work capabilities every 30 days (if no earlier time limit is specified).

9

Creating Functional Job Descriptions

Traditional job descriptions list qualifications, responsibilities, and specific duties, some absolutely necessary and some marginal. These traditional job descriptions rarely address the physical (or mental) abilities needed to perform the job tasks. However, the Americans with Disabilities Act (ADA) and certain state laws prohibiting discrimination against people with disabilities have begun to change job descriptions radically, as employers are being forced to analyze jobs for their essential functions and the physical and mental abilities needed to perform them.

Necessary Elements of Functional Job Descriptions

Employers should analyze all jobs and write corresponding functional job descriptions for each position (see Form 9-1, **Essential Job Functions and Requirements**). These written job descriptions should be completed prior to advertising for, or interviewing, job applicants. The descriptions should identify *essential functions*, or fundamental job duties, and the physical and mental abilities needed to perform these functions. They should also identify any special skills, licensing, or education required.

If an employee spends a large percentage of time performing a particular task, this may be evidence that the task is an essential function. *However, infrequency does not mean that the task is not essential.*

Example Although an airline pilot may land a plane only once during an 8-hour flight, landing is clearly an essential function of the job. Since landing a plane requires depth perception, this physical ability is required to perform the function.

Job descriptions should describe the function by the desired result and avoid prescribing the way that the result is achieved.

Example An essential function of a receptionist is to recognize when people enter an office. This can be accomplished not only by the sighted but also by the blind through a pressure-sensitive doormat that activates a chime when a visitor enters.

Example It would be valid to list "driving a vehicle" as an essential function of a truck-driving position. The position exists because of the function. However, it would not be correct to list "driving a vehicle" as an essential function of an outside sales position, since the ability to personally operate a vehicle is not mandatory for calling on clients. The employee could use public transportation or employ a driver to accomplish this task. An essential function for an outside sales position would be "ability to travel to client sites."

Writing Functional Job Descriptions

The human resources department, safety committee, or workers' comp coordinator (WCC) should assemble a task force to write or review existing job descriptions. Some workers' comp insurers will provide forms and assistance in writing functional job descriptions. Many rehabilitation consultants and occupational health clinics offer this service as well.

One approach is to ask employees (and their supervisors) to complete an analysis of the essential functions required to perform their jobs. The task force can then correlate and combine these results to produce descriptions for each job.

The task force should review all descriptions to see whether any unsafe work practices have been incorporated, such as lifting in excess of recommended limits. If so, redesign the job rather than codify the unsafe activity. In addition, each description should state that the employee must not pose a direct threat to the health or safety of himself/herself or co-workers. Because the job descriptions will influence hiring practices, consider asking an attorney familiar with employment law to review the format and content before officially adopting them.

Functional job descriptions frequently change due to purchase of improved equipment, staff reorganizations, or varied product lines. It is best to review them yearly to keep them current.

Use of Functional Job Description

In addition to serving as a basis for employment decisions (Chapter 10), functional job descriptions form the core of modified-duty assignment programs. It is from these descriptions, and the associated physical abilities required to perform essential functions of particular jobs, that the WCC and supervisor can select more suitable assignments for those returning to work or can devise work accommodations for the regular job assignment.

> **Example** An employee with back pain was ordered by her physician not to return to work because her job involved sitting, a restricted activity. The WCC reviewed the job description, an essential function of which was data input at a computer terminal. Since the employee had no standing or walking limitations, it was a simple modification to install a stand-up computer terminal for her.

Employers should provide health-care professionals with a copy of the injured employee's functional job description to assist in back-to-work decisions. Many health-care professionals are surprised by the big discrepancy between company expectations and the way the employee describes the job!

> **Practical tip** One advantage of having a supervisor accompany an injured worker to the treating health-care professional is that the supervisor is available to explain the organization's transitional work assignment program and answer questions about the injured or ill employee's actual job duties.

Sources of Further Information

Equal Employment Opportunity Commission. *A Technical Assistance Manual on the Employment Provisions (Title I) of the Americans with Disabilities Act.* January 1992. (Call 1-800-669-EEOC for a free copy.)

U.S. Department of Labor, Employment and Training Administration. *Dictionary of Occupational Titles* (4th ed), Vols I and II. Washington, DC, U.S. Government Printing Office, 1991.

Form 9-1, Essential Job Functions and Requirements

Purpose of the Form

- To provide a guide for writing job description
- To assist with employee placement in suitable job
- To guide health-care professionals in making return-to-work decisions
- To assist in making modified-duty assignments

Use of the Form

- When job descriptions are completed, sign, date, and review them annually.
- Provide a copy of an injured employee's job description to the health-care provider at time of the post-injury medical exam.
- Provide a copy of the job description to job applicants and ask whether they can perform the duties listed, with or without reasonable accommodation.

Form 9-1

ESSENTIAL JOB FUNCTIONS AND REQUIREMENTS

Job Title _____

I. Essential Functions (Fundamental Job Duties)

The function may be essential and not marginal if it meets any of these criteria:

1. Does the job exist primarily to perform the function?
2. Are there are a limited number of employees available to perform the function?
3. Is the function highly specialized, requiring expertise or skill to perform it?

_____

_____

_____

_____

_____

_____

_____

_____

_____

_____

_____

II. Education, Training, Experience, Licenses Required

_____

_____

_____

_____

_____

Workers' Comp Management from A to Z: A "How to" Guide with Forms. © Nancy Nivison Menzel, OEM Press, Beverly, MA, 1994.

III. Physical Abilities

These are the physical abilities required to perform the essential functions (fundamental job duties) of this position:

If a physical activity is required, circle how often it is done:

Occasionally: 25% or less of a worker's time
Frequently: More than 25% up to 75% of a worker's time
Continuously: 75% or more of a worker's time

1. Standing	O	C	F
2. Sitting	O	C	F
3. Walking	O	C	F
4. Bending	O	C	F
5. Stooping	O	C	F
6. Twisting	O	C	F
7. Reaching	O	C	F
8. Crouching	O	C	F
9. Crawling	O	C	F
10. Kneeling	O	C	F
11. Climbing	O	C	F
12. Handling (touching or manipulating)	O	C	F
13. Repetitive motion of:			
fingers	O	C	F
wrist	O	C	F
arm/shoulder	O	C	F
leg	O	C	F
foot	O	C	F
14. Pinching	O	C	F

Workers' Comp Management from A to Z: A "How to" Guide with Forms. © Nancy Nivison Menzel, OEM Press, Beverly, MA, 1994.

15.	Lifting under 10 lb	O	C	F
	Lifting 10-20 lb	O	C	F
	Lifting 21-50 lb	O	C	F
	Lifting over 50 lb	O	C	F
16.	Carrying under 10 lb	O	C	F
	Carrying 10-20 lb	O	C	F
	Carrying 21-50	O	C	F
	Carrying over 50 lb	O	C	F
17.	Pushing under 10 lb	O	C	F
	Pushing 10-20 lb	O	C	F
	Pushing 21-50 lb	O	C	F
	Pushing over 50 lb	O	C	F
18.	Pulling under 10 lb	O	C	F
	Pulling 10-20 lb	O	C	F
	Pulling 21-50 lb	O	C	F
	Pulling over 50 lb	O	C	F

19.   Check if job involves any of the following exposures:

☐   Dust

If yes, describe type: _____

☐   Toxic or hazardous substances, including chemicals

If yes, describe: _____

_____

_____

☐   Noise (> 85 dB)

☐   Heat

☐   Cold

☐   Vibration

☐   Biologic hazards (bloodborne pathogens, animal droppings, animal products)

20. Operating machinery or tools (describe)

_____

_____

21. Senses (specify *minimum* requirements)

☐ Vision (acuity, depth perception)

_____

☐ Hearing   _____
☐ Speech   _____
☐ Balance   _____
☐ Other   _____

22. Medical screening

☐ Drugs
☐ Immunities
☐ Department of Transportation physical
☐ Commercial Driver's License exam
☐ Other _____

23. Personal protective equipment required

☐ Gloves (type: _____)
☐ Earplugs
☐ Respirator
☐ Coverall or suit
☐ Safety glasses or goggles
☐ Hard hat
☐ Safety shoes
☐ Other _____

24. Comments or additional requirements:

_____

_____

_____

_____

Job description completed or reviewed by:

_____   _____
(Signature, title)   (Date)

_____   _____
(Signature, title)   (Date)

_____   _____
(Signature, title)   (Date)

10

What You Need to Know about Preplacement Medical Exams

Employees may be hurt on the job due to their inability to meet the demands of the position. Reduce this risk by making sure that new employees are placed in positions that they can physically (and mentally) handle.

Legal Prohibitions Against Pre-employment Tests

The process of having a health-care professional examine a job applicant was formerly called a pre-employment medical exam because it was given prior to hiring. These exams were often broad in nature and reported findings that might have altered the employer's perception of the applicant's ability to perform the job. Since most health-care providers had no description of the actual job requirements, the results were not very relevant for answering the question: "Can this applicant perform the essential functions of this job?"

Employers often made hiring decisions on the results of these exams, unfairly screening out people with disabilities without really considering whether a particular disability would have any effect on job performance. Some employers screened out individuals with disabilities due to fear of increased medical or workers' comp costs or absenteeism. To combat these and other abuses, the Americans with Disabilities Act (ADA) of 1990 prohibited *pre-employment* exams. Under the ADA, employers may conduct only *preplacement, post-offer* medical exams.

Purpose of Preplacement, Post-offer Exams

A "preplacement, post-offer" exam means that only after a candidate has been found to be otherwise qualified (by education, training, credentials, experience, skills, and so forth) for a position and has been offered a job, may the employer require a medical exam to determine the employee's ability to perform the essential functions of the job and to verify that the employee does not pose a significant risk of harm to self or others. An employer can opt not to require any medical exams. However, if an employer does require a preplacement medical exam, it must be required of *all* candidates within that job classification. The job offer can be made contingent on a medical exam to determine if the applicant is capable of performing the *essential functions* of the job.

Now that employers are identifying the abilities needed to perform the essential functions of a job, health-care providers are offering more job-specific exams. Gone are the days when companies established minimum standards (for example, strength requirements) for *all* employees, from clerical workers to laborers. Because the exams have become more focused, the findings have become more useful in preventing occupational injuries and illnesses caused by inappropriate job placement.

Example After a foundry supplied functional job descriptions, the physicians at a local clinic tailored the preplacement exam to test for the ability to perform essential job functions. As a result, the clinic identified an applicant with no depth perception, making it impossible for him to perform an essential function of the job for which he had applied, which involved pouring molten metal from shoulder height to a bucket on the floor. Since it was not easy to modify the job, he was offered another position that did not require depth perception.

The health-care professional conducting the medical exam should also report whether the candidate's physical (or mental) condition poses a significant threat to the health or safety of self or others.

Example An applicant for a job as a baggage handler who suffers from occasional epileptic seizures may pose a safety hazard to self and others when driving a baggage cart. However, before turning down such an applicant, the employer must consider many things, including the validity of the medical information, whether a reasonable accommodation could be made to eliminate the safety hazard, or if there are other jobs available in which the applicant's medical condition would not pose a risk.

In addition to providing guidance to the employer about whether a job candidate is physically suited for a particular job, preplacement physical exams also provide baseline data that may prove helpful if a workers' comp claim is filed later. Most states' workers' comp laws require rehabilitation only to the level of physical functioning prior to a job-related injury or illness.

With baseline data provided by preplacement exams, post-injury impairment ratings for settlement purposes can be based on the level of functioning at the time of hire, not optimum physical functioning.

In addition, many states have established *second-injury funds* that help to reduce the risks of hiring an employee with a disability. These funds are intended to spread the cost of re-injuries over all employers. Establishing a medical baseline at the time of hire may assist in making claims against this fund if re-injury occurs.

In addition, the ADA allows inquiries about past workers' comp injuries during the post-offer exam. In some states, an applicant who misrepresents his or her physical condition at the time of hire may be ineligible for workers' comp payments.

Preparing for the Exam

Give the health-care professional a copy of all functional job descriptions for positions subject to preplacement medical exams and a **Report of Preplacement Medical Exam** (Form 10-1) for use in reporting results of the exam. Ask for and review a detailed description of the proposed exam to make sure it is appropriate for the job. Some physical therapy departments are able to simulate many jobs and observe a candidate's ability to perform tasks. The one quality that is not usually tested is endurance, since these exams last, at most, an hour.

Implementing a Pre-employment Drug Testing Program

Employees who abuse drugs are thought to have accidents at a higher rate due to impaired senses, memory, reasoning, and judgment. Many employers now require pre-employment drug tests to try to screen out individuals predisposed to accidents due to the use of illegal drugs or the illicit use of legal drugs. Since drug tests are not considered medical exams, and using amphetamines, cannabinoids, cocaine, opiates and phencyclidine (PCP) is illegal, the ADA does not prohibit pre-employment drug screening. At a minimum, drug screening identifies potential job candidates who are able to abstain from drugs at least long enough to get hired.

The employer does not have to demonstrate a job-related reason for drug testing. Although pre-employment drug testing is allowed, it is more cost-effective to do drug screening after a job offer has been made, since this will mean fewer tests.

Because of the complexity of administering and interpreting drug tests properly, employers should seek both legal and medical advice before setting up a drug-screening program. Employers should also verify that the testing facility is using proper collection techniques and documents chain of custody when sending specimens to an approved laboratory. All results should be interpreted by a physician, who can decide the validity of any positive result in light of legitimate medications the employee may be taking.

Some employers require drug tests for current employees who apply to transfer to another department. Other employers conduct random drug testing or drug testing after accidents. Employers who wish to establish, or are required by the U.S. Department of Transportation or other regulators to establish, such post-hiring programs should seek legal assistance before proceeding.

Practical tip Post a sign in a prominent place and print on the application for employment that prospective employees are subject to pre-employment drug testing. This will discourage drug abusers from applying for employment.

Recordkeeping Requirements and Disclosure Restrictions

EMPLOYERS

The ADA specifies that any information on the medical condition of an applicant must be collected on, and stored in, separate files and treated as confidential by employers, except for possible disclosure to supervisors regarding needed restrictions and accommodations. In addition, certain conditions can be disclosed to first-aid and safety personnel who might have a need to know to provide help. Finally, the medical record can be disclosed to government officials looking into compliance with the ADA and to state workers' comp second-injury funds.

HEALTH-CARE PROFESSIONALS

Disclosure restrictions limit health-care professionals to providing summary statements regarding the applicant's ability to perform the essential functions of the job in question, with or without accommodation. When selecting a health-care provider for administering post-offer medical exams, employers should ask to see a copy of the form on which the provider reports results, to check compliance with these restrictions. *The health-care provider is an agent of the employer; hence, the employer is liable for the provider's actions.*

If the health professional's medical report indicates that the applicant can perform the essential functions of the job with accommodation, the employer determines whether the needed accommodation is "reasonable," given the resources of the employer. Most job accommodations can be made inexpensively.

Example A hospital's safety department analyzed accidents and found a high incidence of back injuries to new employees assigned to the rehabilitation unit, where many patients had to be lifted out of beds and chairs. The preplacement medical exam was modified to more carefully evaluate muscle tone and lifting strength for these jobs. Most job applicants failed to meet the level needed to perform the essential functions of the job. As an accommodation, the unit put in more mechanical lifts and increased staff to provide for two-person lifting. In addition, the physical therapy department put new rehabilitation-unit employees through a 2-week work-hardening program prior to assignment. As a result, the incidence of back injuries dropped dramatically.

Employers can receive free information and expert consultation on hiring persons with disabilities, making an accommodation, or general compliance with the ADA by calling the Job Accommodation Network (JAN) at 1-800-ADA-WORK or 1-800-JAN-7234.

Practical tip Because the ADA, state workers' comp laws, and state disability discrimination laws overlap, with sometimes conflicting provisions, employers should have an attorney review their hiring practices for legality.

Sources of Further Information

Goldenthal N. *Understanding the Americans with Disabilities Act: A Compliance Guide for Health Professionals and Employers.* Beverly, MA, OEM Press, 1993.

Walsh JM, Gust SW (eds). *Workplace Drug Abuse Policy: Considerations and Experience in the Business Community.* National Institute on Drug Abuse, Department of Health and Human Services, Public Health Service, Alcohol, Drug Abuse, and Mental Health Administration, 1989.

Form 10-1, Report of Preplacement Medical Exam

Purpose of Form

- To standardize the reporting of preplacement exams
- To raise the awareness of health-care providers of the need to evaluate abilities in light of job requirements
- To ensure that no confidential medical information is inappropriately disclosed
- To alert employers to the need for accommodation of individuals with disabilities who can (with accommodation) perform essential functions of the job

Use of Form

- Use the form as a standard to compare against the form that the company's health-care provider is now using.
- In the event of a workers' comp claim, advise the insurer that a preplacement baseline medical record exists.
- If the health-care provider finds an applicant not qualified to perform the essential functions of the job, consider the reasons carefully or seek legal advice before turning down an applicant.
- If an applicant with a disability needs an accommodation to perform the job, consider whether that accommodation is reasonable.

Form 10-1

REPORT OF PREPLACEMENT MEDICAL EXAM

TO: (company name) _____

I have examined (employee name) _____

of (address) _____

for the ability to perform the essential functions of the following job:_____

_____. I have read the job description for this position.

This person

☐   is qualified to perform the essential functions of the job, with or without

accommodation. Accommodation needed, if any: _____

_____

☐   is not qualified to perform the essential functions of the job, with or without

accommodation for the following reason: _____

_____

A record of this confidential medical examination is on file at:

_____
(name of facility and address)

_____   _____
(signature and credentials)   (date)

11

Implementing a Modified-Duty Program

Modified duty is the single most effective way to rehabilitate workers, keep them connected to the workplace, and reduce the cost of claims through indemnity savings and increased productivity.

Terminology

There are many terms for temporarily altering an employee's job to accommodate changes in abilities. Some of these terms are "light duty," "modified duty," "alternative assignment," "transitional work," and "work hardening." Many employers avoid using the term "light duty" because it may imply that the job is not important or may give the impression to co-workers that the injured employee is being rewarded for injury. Whatever it is called, every day that an injured employee is brought in to work is a day that both indemnity costs go down and productivity goes up.

Essential Components of the Program

Before implementing a modified-duty (transitional work) program, the company should have completed its functional job descriptions, chosen designated medical providers who support modified duty, appointed a workers' compensation coordinator (WCC), and put in place policies that encourage the early return to work of those with work-related injuries or illnesses. After these steps, management should educate supervisors on the reasons for, and benefits of, modified duty for both the employee and supervisor. In addition to promoting recovery, modified duty is an opportunity to provide cross training, allowing more flexibility in later job assignments.

Ways To Modify the Work Assignment

Some of the variables that may be modified are:

- Length of time at work (fewer hours/day)
- Number of days per week (fewer days/week)
- Job assignment (e.g., from "driver" to "receptionist")
- Job description (removing or adding tasks)
- Task modification (e.g., lifting limits)
- Responsibilities (e.g., supervisor to staff)
- Productivity rate (e.g., fewer units per day)

The WCC needs to be creative, innovative, and persevering to find suitable assignments and should ask supervisors, the employee, and other employees for suggestions.

Things to avoid:

- "Make work" or idle assignments
- Any appearance of punishment
- Assignments beyond the employee's skill or ability level
- Paying for off-premises "work hardening," when similar therapeutic activities can be incorporated in a modified-duty assignment

Example An employee at a grocery distribution center strained his back. The physician permitted modified duty with a lifting limit of 2 lb. The supervisor brought the injured employee back to the warehouse but required him to sit in the employee break area for 8 hours. The injured employee felt punished and useless. The other employees resented their co-worker for being rewarded with an "easy" assignment while they were hard at work. They petitioned their union to add a "no light duty" clause to the next collective bargaining agreement. Some decided to "strain" their backs as well, to get a respite from their physically demanding jobs.

Things to include:

- Productive work when possible
- Tasks that incorporate required physical conditioning or work hardening

- Flexibility to allow compliance with treatment program
- Asking the employee for suggestions of modified duties
- Retention of previous pay rate

Example While a stockroom employee was recovering from an inguinal hernia repair, his lifting was not to exceed 5 lb. He was temporarily reassigned as an order packer, with another employee removing filled boxes from the work bench.

Example A surgical-instrument assembler slipped on the employer's premises and fractured her ankle. A physician set the fracture under anesthesia and ordered her away from work for 4 weeks. At the next visit, he changed her cast and again ordered her away from work for another month. When the Human Resources secretary observed that the employee could drive to work to pick up her extended benefits check and to the market to shop, she contacted the physician and described a bench-work assignment that the employee could do sitting with her leg extended. As a result, he revised her work restrictions to include 4 hours of modified duty daily, which was later extended to 8 hours a day for the final month of her convalescence.

Example An employee was ordered to have frequent and lengthy physical therapy treatments aimed at improving shoulder mobility and strength. The WCC called the physical therapist for a description of the exercise routine and incorporated it in a modified-duty assignment involving reaching, lifting, and shoulder rotation. The therapy was reduced to once a week, with the employee able to work the rest of the time.

Practical tip If the company has many employees on modified duty who are receiving physical therapy, the WCC should consider equipping a room to allow on-site therapy. Another possibility is paying for a nearby health-club membership for recovering employees, which allows them to carry out most exercise programs much less expensively than at an occupational rehabilitation clinic.

Procedure for Initiating a Modified-Duty Assignment and Follow-up

The WCC should ask the health-care provider for a written release for modified duty, with the employee's restrictions and abilities spelled out. This serves as the foundation for selecting an appropriate assignment.

After the WCC has reviewed work restrictions with the employee's supervisor and they have jointly written a **Description of Modified-Duty Assignment** (Form 11-2), the WCC should provide it, together with an **Employee Notice of Modified-Duty Assignment** (Form 11-1), to the employee, so that there is no misunderstanding about starting dates and duties. It is sometimes helpful to write out a schedule, including stretch breaks and exercises, if they have been ordered. The assignment should be clearly identified as temporary (a maximum of 30 days). See Figure 11-1 for a sample description of a modified-duty assignment.

This assignment has been selected to accommodate the following restrictions: _prolonged sitting, lifting, and endurance._

   I. **Primary Functions**
      Assist in producing glass fiber
      Assist in inspecting finished glass fiber
      Assist with maintaining safe workplace

  II. **Duties and Responsibilities**
      1. Check material-delivery invoices against existing material inventories and usage. Notify Purchasing of discrepancies.
      2. Monitor control room alarms.
      3. Verify in-shop MSDS books against hazardous materials list.
      4. Visually inspect quality of strand as it enters winders.
      5. Clean and check respirators in Mix Room according to written protocol.
      6. Verify fire extinguishers and hoses for proper operation, location, and documentation.
      7. Check for presence, accuracy, and legibility of all chemical labels.
      8. Clean Mix Room vats (automated soaking, draining, drying).
      9. Relieve fiber formers.
     10. Load, run, and empty dryers.

 III. **Schedule**
Mornings (7:30-11:30) 5 days a week. Take stretch break for 10 minutes at 9 a.m. and 10:30 a.m. Do not sit for more than 1 hour at a time. Report to supervisor if any activities cause increased symptoms.

  IV. **Authorized by:**

 _____   _____
 signature, title   date

Fig. 11-1. Sample Description of Modified-Duty Assignment

Once the employee has returned to work, the WCC should check periodically with the employee and supervisor to make sure that the modified-duty assignment remains appropriate. The fact that an employee may not like the work or finds it boring is not sufficient reason to change it. In fact, job boredom often motivates employees to hasten their convalescence so that they can return to their regular jobs.

After 30 days (or sooner, if there has been an intervening appointment with the health care provider), the WCC and supervisor should revise the modified-duty assignment to take advantage of any progress in abilities or lessening of restrictions. If several months elapse with no improvement in the employee's work abilities nor a release from the health-care provider for modified work, the diagnosis or treatment may be incorrect. The WCC should insist on a second medical opinion.

If lack of recovery progress persists after exhausting all treatment options, the WCC should discuss with the insurance adjuster whether to settle the case, offer vocational rehabilitation, or make a permanent job accommodation, since the employee may have reached maximum medical improvement. Under no circumstances should the same temporary modified-duty assignment be continued indefinitely, since the employee will not be motivated to improve and may be able to make a strong case that the employer has permanently modified the job duties.

Practical tip The WCC can ask the recovering employee to sign a rehabilitation agreement that specifies what actions the employee agrees to take to achieve recovery milestones; for example, performing prescribed exercises until achieving a specified range of joint motion. The WCC should review and revise this agreement every 30 days.

Overcoming Resistance to the Program and Problems

Despite the best preparation, the WCC will often find that supervisors, injured employees, and health-care providers are initially reluctant to cooperate with the modified-duty program. Supervisors will often state flatly, "I don't have any work that someone who can't lift (or climb or bend or reach) can do." Employees may say, "If I can't do my regular job, I don't want to come in." Health-care providers may refuse to clear an employee for work because they are thinking, "I'm afraid the patient will aggravate the injury and sue me!"

The WCC will have to address each party's concerns and motives before succeeding with the program. Supervisors can be motivated to participate by applying economic penalties against that department's budget for every absent employee or by providing productivity incentives.

The WCC can persuade injured employees by providing reassurances that the assignment will promote recovery and may result in a bigger paycheck than indemnity alone, which is a set percentage of an employee's regular pay. The WCC should be sensitive to underlying problems or obstacles that the employee may have difficulty expressing due to embarrassment, pride, or fear.

Example A hotel housekeeper had a 6-week absence due to a back injury. When released for modified duty, she resisted coming in by complaining of increased pain. The WCC tried to find the source of the reluctance, possibly lack of transportation or child care. Neither was a problem. After some gentle questioning, the WCC learned that the housekeeper had gained weight, had no uniforms to fit her, and no money to buy larger ones. The WCC sent her new uniforms, and the housekeeper reported for duty the next day.

The WCC will have to earn the trust and confidence of the health-care provider by describing safeguards in the modified-duty program that will prevent re-injury, such as written assignments and supervisor training. The WCC should send a copy of the transitional assignment to the health-care provider for review.

If a health-care provider repeatedly refuses to release an employee for modified work, ask specifically what items on the list of duties the employee is incapable of performing and why. Ask uncooperative providers if they would keep their own employee with a similar injury out for this length of time. If lack of cooperation continues, the WCC can ask the insurance adjuster to intervene. Sometimes a hint that the insurer is going to investigate the claim for overuse of medical services is enough to produce "miracle cures."

If an employee refuses to accept a modified-duty assignment for which he or she has been medically cleared, report this to the insurance adjuster for possible denial of benefits. In these situations, the employee usually locates a new, more "sympathetic" provider who again delays any return to work. To address this problem, some states' workers' comp laws have provisions prohibiting "doctor-shopping." However, if an employee is determined to stretch out the case, it often seems that nothing is effective, resulting in frustration for the WCC.

Example A new employee at a mailing-service company reported that she had hurt her back when kicking a bag of letters across the floor. She went to a hospital emergency room, where the physician on duty gave her muscle relaxants and ordered her to stay out of work for 1 week. When the WCC called her, her father answered all calls by stating that she was sleeping and unable to come to the phone. At the end of 2 weeks, she had not returned to work nor had she consulted a second physician. During this time, she had been spotted by co-workers swimming at a community pool. The insurance adjuster told the employer to give the claimant time to locate a new doctor and that the claimant reported swimming was therapy for her back. After 3 weeks, the employee retained a physician who continued the "no work" order, referred her to physical therapy, and scheduled a battery of expensive tests, most of which the employee postponed at least twice for varied reasons. When these tests were finally completed weeks later, they proved negative, and the physician cleared her for modified duty. However, the employee refused to sign for a mailed copy of her modified-duty assignment and sought a new doctor. The adjuster refused the employer's request for an independent medical exam (IME), stating that she preferred to await the opinion of the new physician to save claim administration dollars. After 4 months and more (negative) tests, the third physician cleared the employee to return to work. She then switched to a chiropractor who began "spinal manipulations" and sent word that the employee would be unable to work for at least 4 more weeks. At this point, the adjuster filed to discontinue benefits. The employee hired a lawyer, who appealed the insurer's action. The case then entered the process of dispute resolution at the state's department of industrial accidents.

Practical tip If you feel that the insurance adjuster is mishandling a case, request a conference with the adjuster's supervisor to review whether the adjuster is following proper procedures.

Sources of Further Information

For help in returning an employee to work after an injury or illness, call the Job Accommodation Network (JAN) at 1-800-ADA-WORK for possible solutions.

Call ABLEDATA at 1-800-227-0216 for information about adaptive devices for all disabilities.

Form 11-1, Employee Notice of Modified-Duty Assignment

Purpose of Form

- To provide notice to the employee of modified-work assignment
- To provide a written record that the assignment is temporary and transitional

Use of Form

- With the completed form in hand, discuss the assignment with the employee.
- If the discussion is by telephone, mail a copy of the form to the employee. If the discussion is in person, provide a copy to the employee at the time of the meeting.
- Include a detailed description of the duties, hours, and responsibilities (Form 11-2).
- Put both forms in a tickler file for review in 30 days.

Form 11-1

EMPLOYEE NOTICE OF MODIFIED-DUTY ASSIGNMENT

Date:_____

Dear _____ ,

We have received the good news that your health-care provider, _____ , has recommended your return to work. In accordance with company policy, which encourages an early return to work, your job will be modified until you reach full recovery. We are offering you a temporary, transitional work assignment to accommodate your current restrictions and abilities, which are:

_____

_____

Please review the enclosed Description of Modified-Duty Assignment for more details.

Your schedule is as follows:

Beginning date: _____

Shift: _____

Hours per day: _____   Hours per week: _____

Pay rate: _____ .

Please call me at (tel. #) _____ by (date) _____ to verify your return to work in this transitional, modified-duty work assignment, which we will re-evaluate in 30 days (or sooner). Thank you.

Sincerely yours,

_____
Workers' Compensation Coordinator

Workers' Comp Management from A to Z: A "How to" Guide with Forms. © Nancy Nivison Menzel, OEM Press, Beverly, MA, 1994.

Form 11-2, Description of Modified-Duty Assignment

Purpose of Form

- To summarize restrictions and selected activities
- To reassure the employee's health-care provider about the safety of the assignment
- To serve as a benchmark for measuring the employee's progress in recovery

Use of Form

- The employee's supervisor and the WCC jointly write specifics of the modified-duty assignment.
- Send a copy of the written assignment to the employee's health-care provider together with a copy of the Employee Notice (Form 11-1).
- Every 30 days, review the assignment and modify it, if appropriate (based on the health-care provider's recommendation).
- If, in 30 days, there is no improvement in work restrictions, seek a second medical opinion.

Form 11-2

DESCRIPTION OF MODIFIED-DUTY ASSIGNMENT

This assignment has been selected to accommodate the following restrictions:

_____

I. **Primary Functions**

II. **Duties and Responsibilities**

III. **Schedule**

IV. **Authorized by:**

_____   _____

signature, title   date

12

Choosing an Outside Health-Care Provider

Patti E. Walkover, MS, RN

In this era of corporate downsizing, more and more large companies are abolishing their in-house medical departments, which were once staffed with company physicians and nurses. Smaller companies have always been unable to afford on-site physician services, so organizations of all sizes are now seeking competent outside health-care providers.

The appropriate choice of an outside health-care provider or panel of providers is critical to the success of any employer's workers' comp cost-containment effort. The health-care provider plays a pivotal role in a company's ability to access information, exercise control, and return an employee to work. How providers operate their business and how they are perceived by injured or ill employees may likewise have a direct impact on return to work.

Criteria for Evaluating Potential Health-Care Providers

To determine a health-care provider's ability to participate in your program, thoroughly evaluate, at a minimum, the following issues:

- Level of experience and expertise in the diagnosis and treatment of work-related injuries and illnesses
- Working relationships with specialty providers, particularly orthopedists
- Knowledge of applicable state workers' comp legislation

- Demonstrated early-return-to-work philosophy and practice
- Attitude toward company/payer as a "client"
- Appropriateness of internal as well as external referral patterns for specialists, diagnostic procedures, physical therapy, and other services
- Existence of business relationships that could lead to questionable referral and utilization patterns, such as provider's ownership of physical therapy practices, imaging centers, pharmacies, and other optional services
- Comprehensiveness of services at or near the clinic's location, such as radiologic (x-ray) and laboratory services offered on site
- Convenience and accessibility of the provider's location to employer and employees
- Hours of service that are compatible with the needs of the company and employees
- Twenty-four-hour, 7-days-a-week coverage provided either directly or in coordinated manner through an emergency department
- Willingness to provide some services at the employer's site, such as vaccinations or back-injury prevention programs

Each issue plays an important role in the effectiveness of a health-care provider or organization. Many are self-explanatory. Key issues are discussed in greater detail below.

Finding Qualified, Experienced Providers

The practice of occupational health is a specialty not unlike orthopedics, cardiology, or pediatrics. There are physicians and nurse practitioners experienced in occupational health who understand mechanisms of injury, workplace exposures, injury prevention, modified duty, and symptom magnification. They will visit the workplace to understand a company's work environment, the type of work its employees do, and the jobs that are available. When an employee becomes injured or ill, they work in partnership with the employer to return the employee to work as soon as possible, based on their understanding of the specific workplace. Occupational health professionals are active proponents of modified-duty programs and may even help an organization develop an effective program if asked.

These professionals are generally found in practice at occupational health centers that operate independently or as hospital-based programs. However, they also may be in private practice or members of large multispecialty physician groups.

Occupational health physicians come from a variety of clinical backgrounds, including family practice, internal medicine, and emergency medicine. Board certification in occupational medicine (preventive medicine) is available and pursued by many interested physicians, but it is still not extremely prevalent. Physicians must complete additional education and training programs before being allowed to take the certification exam. Therefore, a board-certified occupational medicine physician may be difficult to find. Contacting the American College of Occupational and Environmental Medicine (ACOEM) may prove helpful (see "Sources of Further Information").

Some nurse practitioners have completed additional training in occupational health or have had many years of experience in this field. Each state regulates the extent to which these practitioners can operate independently, but many offer more convenient and lower cost care for less serious cases than hospital outpatient clinics or emergency rooms.

Chiropractors often advertise their expertise in treating workers' comp cases, particularly back and neck injuries. However, chiropractors do not provide care for the full spectrum of occupational injuries and illnesses and are less suitable as an employer's primary health-care provider.

Selecting Primary Providers with Specialty-Provider Networks

Whenever possible, an employer should opt for a health-care provider with an integrated program, including an appropriate network of specialists. This means that the primary provider has working relationships with specialists who are knowledgeable in occupational health, understand the needs of the employee and employer, and will make an effort to get the employee back to work. It also means that the specialist is willing to schedule appointments in a timely manner (within 48 hours of a request) to facilitate case resolution. Without these relationships, it is not uncommon for an orthopedic appointment for a nonacute evaluation to take 4 weeks to schedule. Among unrelated providers, an employee may be returned to temporary duty by the primary provider only to have the referral specialist put the employee out of work.

Communication between health-care professionals is as critical to the success of a cost-containment program as is communication with the employer. If a program lacks coordination, the injured or ill employee can lose precious recovery time, while becoming disheartened and confused by the lack of continuity in treatment.

Demonstrated Early-Return-To-Work Philosophy and Practice

While injury and illness prevention provides the ultimate in cost containment, in the event an injury or illness occurs, early return to work to full or modified duty offers the next best solution. This is due in large part to the fact that more than half of an employer's workers' comp dollars is spent on indemnity (wage replacement), not on medical payments. To be successful in cost containment, health-care providers must understand the importance of early-return-to-work to the well-being of the employee and must work in partnership with the employer to develop safe and reasonable early-return-to-work options.

In some situations, a case manager from an insurance carrier, workers' comp managed-care company, or other source will be responsible for intervening with a medical provider who has not offered an appropriate return to work. While this can serve as a necessary means of monitoring the medical provider, changing a return-to-work date after the fact can cause the employee to be confused and angry and possibly to seek legal action.

Example A nursing-home employee injured her back and went to her personal physician who put her on bed rest and muscle relaxants for a week and scheduled a revisit in 1 week. The nursing home had developed a modified-duty program that included jobs for individuals who could do no lifting. A few days after the visit, the case manager received information on the case. He contacted the physician, described the modified duty, and received a revised return-to-work note from the physician indicating that the employee could return to the modified-duty job. When the employee was notified of the change, she was confused and became irate. She complained to her physician about this change. As a result, the physician referred her to an orthopedic specialist for further evaluation and kept her off work until her orthopedic appointment.

In the above example, the result would have been very different if the personal physician had known prior to seeing the injured employee that temporary work was available and the employee had not become confused and made to feel manipulated. Most employees with legitimate work-related injuries or illnesses want to comply and return to work. However, even the most compliant employee will object to this type of change in their work status after the initial determination has been made.

If you choose health-care providers who believe in early return to work and are knowledgeable about jobs in your company, you will increase compliance with these efforts and not antagonize your employees. In evaluating providers specifically for their return-to-work philosophy and practice, a detailed discussion should let you know how they think. Ask what is the average length of time away from work for cases they have treated with the following diagnoses:

- Low back strain
- Carpal tunnel syndrome
- Hand laceration requiring sutures
- Foreign body in eye

If the provider does not know the average lost time, this indicates a lack of control over, or disinterest in, outcomes. If lost time for either of the first two conditions exceeds more than a few days before release to modified duty, ask why. If either of the latter two conditions results in lost time beyond the day of injury, this exceeds the norm and should be explained.

Ask for and examine their case-documentation procedures, return-to-work forms, and methods of communication with you as well as with the employee and insurer. It is in your best interest as an employer to insist on immediate feedback on medical findings and work status, preferably by a telephone call from the treating physician or other health-care provider. Carefully check references from several client companies.

Attitude Toward Company/Payer as "Client"

Traditional health-care providers may have difficulty understanding that the company/payer is a client, as is the employee. This can be especially true if the medical provider chosen by a company is also the primary-care provider many employees use for non-work-related injuries and illnesses (i.e., their family doctor). Occupational health programs whose practice is limited to work-related issues will not have this conflict of interest and may prove to be more satisfactory partners.

Provider Utilization and Referral Patterns

Medical costs account for the next largest proportion (more than 40%) of workers' comp dollars and can best be controlled through appropriate utilization of medical services. This is particularly true in states with fee schedules (set maximums per service), since providers may compensate for a decrease in reimbursement with an increase in utilization.

Example An employee with work-related intermittent low back pain consulted a physician during an office visit, for which the state has prescribed a maximum payment of $40. At the time of the initial visit, the physician ordered radiographs (x-rays) and 6 weeks of physical therapy, both provided by facilities that the physician owned. These services appeared to be overtreatment in light of the mild nature of the employee's symptoms. However, the physician was able to profit by taking advantage of the lack of provisions for utilization review in that state's workers' comp law.

Individuals trained in case management and utilization management can assist you in spotting overutilization and inappropriate use of tests and referrals. However, if you begin with a provider who currently practices with appropriate utilization, you are able to avoid potential problems before they occur.

Historically, most utilization review has been performed primarily as a bill-auditing function well after care has been rendered. A truly effective cost-containment program requires a shift to utilization management that occurs concurrently with treatment and is designed to have an impact on the course of treatment.

The medical provider you evaluate should give you information on the treatment of specific diagnoses. Clinical pathways (treatment protocols) are being developed by many providers (and some state workers' comp regulators) to ensure consistency as well as proper utilization. Request the clinical guidelines that a prospective medical provider uses in his or her workers' comp practice.

> **Example** An electronics-assembly employer with a high incidence of carpal tunnel syndrome among its work force sought an occupational health clinic that supported a conservative approach to treatment. Any providers who mentioned surgery as an early treatment option were excluded from further consideration.

Comprehensiveness of the Clinical Facility and Location

The injured employee's perception of the circumstances of the care he or she receives is as important as the actual quality of the medical care. Employees may not be in a position to judge the treatment they receive, but those employees will know that it took 20 minutes to find a parking place and that they had to register several different times and travel to three separate locations to complete diagnostic tests. The comprehensiveness of the clinical facility and its convenience are key factors that contribute to the success of an employer's efforts to get employees to use a company-designated provider.

Injured or ill employees sent for treatment at a company-chosen medical-provider site arrive in an adversarial state. They have been injured or made ill by their job, and they have been sent to a physician not of their choosing. If, on top of these drawbacks, they are sent to a medical provider who is less than "user-friendly," program compliance will suffer. Health-care providers who do not provide easy access and hassle-free visits will also create an additional burden for the employer, due to the excessive time off work that employees spend in the medical provider's office.

The evaluation of potential medical providers is an involved but necessary process. The **Checklist for Selection of Health-Care Provider(s)** (Form 12-1) will help focus and standardize your search. Once you have selected leading health-provider candidates, ask them to read and sign a **Letter Supporting Modified Duty** (Form 12-2).

Preferred Provider Organizations

Preferred provider organizations (PPOs) are groups of independent medical providers, hospitals, and other providers of medical services (e.g., radiology, pharmacy, durable medical equipment) brought together by an unrelated entity (e.g., insurance carrier, managed-care company, major employer) for the purpose of providing services to a select group of covered individuals. PPOs are becoming increasingly popular for workers' comp cases, particularly in non-fee-schedule states where PPOs offer discounted rates on medical services. The entity marketing the PPO obtains discounts from PPO member organizations and then sells this discount to the employer or payer, keeping a percentage of the discount for itself. The attraction in this PPO model is the convenience of a preexisting network and a discount. However, PPOs offering only discounted fee arrangements in the absence of utilization management, case management, or comprehensive managed-care services will not help you achieve your goal of cost containment. Any potential solution that focuses only on part of the problem (medical costs) without also including the rest of the problem (lost time and other indemnity issues) will leave you short of your goal.

Self-insured employers may do as well as, or better than, an outside PPO by contacting their local hospital and directly negotiating favorable rates not only for treatment of workers' comp injuries and illnesses, but also other health services. Insurers routinely receive discounts of up to 30% on a hospital's standard rates yet pass along only part of that to their clients. Most hospitals and medical providers are eager to work directly with the employer to eliminate the middleperson and gain preferred-provider status. In return, the employer must structure its health-benefits plan to provide employees with financial incentives to go to designated facilities. However, choosing an outside PPO may be beneficial for employers with multiple locations over a large geographic area, as many PPOs operate in several states.

PPOs operating in fee-schedule states may also offer discounts and are likely to charge via an access fee that is often presented as a capitated (per employee) rate but may be based on actual utilization. Choosing a PPO in a fee-schedule state carries the same disadvantages as those in a non-fee schedule state if the emphasis is only on medical costs and not also on the other important elements of cost containment.

Choosing a PPO is no different from choosing an individual medical provider. The issues addressed above should be answered by the PPO. You should request and receive information about credentials, quality assurance, medical protocols, and policies and procedures used by the PPO, as well as specific information about the providers in the network that you are most likely to use. If you choose a PPO, be sure that its provider network includes the physicians that you need in the treatment and management of work-related issues. Many PPOs begin as group-health PPOs and simply convert all of their physicians to workers' comp. In such PPOs, you are likely to see as many pediatricians listed as orthopedic surgeons.

Only you can decide on the best medical-provider option for your company, based on your individual needs. Individual providers, clinics, hospital-based programs, and PPOs all have their place. Your job is to identify your needs, evaluate provider options in your geographic area, and put together the obvious match. But whether you look to an individual provider or a PPO, perform a careful and complete evaluation. Your medical provider must be a partner and an ally and part of a total commitment to workers' comp cost containment.

Sources of Further Information

Official Journal of the American Association of Occupational Health Nurses, Slack Incorporated, 6900 Grove Road, Thorofare, NJ 08086-9447; tel. (609) 848-1000. (Publishes list of nurse consultants semiannually; accepts employment advertising.)

AAOHN NEWS, American Association of Occupational Health Nurses, 50 Lenox Pointe, Atlanta, GA 30324-3176; tel. (800) 241-8014. (Monthly newsletter that accepts employment advertising.)

American Board for Occupational Health Nurses, 10503 North Cedarburg Road, Mequon, WI 53092-4403; tel. (414)242-0704. (Provides list of certified occupational health nurses [COHNs] by state.)

The American College of Occupational and Environmental Medicine (ACOEM), 55 West Seegers Road, Arlington Heights, IL, 60005. (Provides list of board-certified occupational medicine physicians.)

Data Link Research, P.O. Box 141, Fair Oaks, CA 95628. (Directory of occupational health centers.)

Form 12-1, Checklist for Selection of Health-Care Provider(s)

Purpose of Form

- To standardize the process of selecting a designated provider
- To ensure that all important questions are asked of potential health-care providers
- To highlight possible problem areas, such as a provider's ownership of an on-site pharmacy
- To remind potential providers that the employer is closely scrutinizing their services

Use of Form

- Make an appointment with the provider to discuss questions on the form.
- Note number and credentials of staff (e.g., three RNs [BSNs], one multimodality technician [x-ray and lab], one full-time MD with board certification in family practice, two part-time MDs with board certification in emergency medicine).
- The more "yes" answers, the more favorable the overall score, with the exception that a "yes" for a financial interest in physical therapy, imaging, or pharmacy services is a potential negative.
- Interview the ranking physician or nurse practitioner to determine his/her commitment to modified duty and to convey the essence of the employer's program.
- Review answers from several providers to select the one most suitable for meeting the employer's needs.

Form 12-1

CHECKLIST FOR SELECTION OF HEALTH-CARE PROVIDER(S)

Name of provider	Telephone

Address

☐ Private Practice   ☐ Group Practice   ☐ Private Clinic   ☐ Hospital Clinic
☐ PPO Network Member   ☐ Other:

Licensures, certifications, and specialties of staff (include total numbers of each):

☐ Ambulatory, nonserious cases only   ☐ Full service, including catastrophic care

Days and hours of service:

Describe provision for after-hours coverage:

Is telephone call required prior to sending injured employee? ☐ yes ☐ no
If yes, telephone number and name of contact person:

	Yes	No
Experienced in care of workers' comp injuries and illnesses		
Willing to complete Medical Treatment Report (Form 16-2) at time of service		
Immediate follow-up telephone call if necessary to add to above		
Written treatment protocols available for review		
Demonstrated early-return-to-work philosophy and practice		
Keeps clients' job descriptions on file for reference		
Maintains periodic contact with referral specialists on cases		
Knowledgeable about workers' comp law		
Radiologic and clinical laboratory on site or nearby		
Referral-provider patterns appear appropriate		
Physician in charge or on call has hospital-admitting privileges		
Documentation (provider notes, test results) organized and clear		
Other clients give good references		
Staff members bilingual in:		
Has financial interest in physical therapy/imaging center or pharmacy		
Close proximity and easy access, parking		
Rapid registration procedures		
Within 5 miles of nearest hospital		
Other:		

Summary of physician interview: _____

References contacted: _____

_____   _____
Signed   Date

Workers' Comp Management from A to Z: A "How to" Guide with Forms. © Nancy Nivison Menzel, OEM Press, Beverly, MA, 1994.

Form 12-2, Letter Supporting Modified Duty

Purpose of Form

- To serve as reminder to health-care providers of the employer's early-return-to-work program
- To state employer's expectations in clear language
- To provide an opportunity for discussion of issues with provider(s) before service begins
- To periodically evaluate a provider's delivery of services

Use of Form

- Provide a copy to designated health-care providers.
- Ask that the ranking health-care professional review its contents and sign it, if in agreement.
- Note promptness of return; delayed responses can indicate later communication problems.
- Keep a copy on file, with notes on service quality, for annual review.

Workers' Comp Management from A to Z

Form 12-2

LETTER SUPPORTING MODIFIED DUTY

Dear Employer:

I have reviewed your policy statement on workers injured on the job, which encourages the return of employees to alternative-duty assignments at the earliest time that it is medically possible for them to do so.

I will support this early-return-to-work policy by:

- encouraging employees to return to work by focusing on abilities and rehabilitation.

- reviewing an employee's job description prior to making a fitness-for-work decision.

- specifying medical restrictions or physical limitations.

- suggesting appropriate modified duties.

- promptly completing the Medical Treatment Report (Form 16-2).

- communicating with you on case status as needed.

If I restrict an employee from work entirely, I will re-evaluate the employee for modified-duty capability at each revisit and will provide an estimated return-to-work date whenever possible.

_____   _____
(Signature)   (Date)

_____
(Name of organization)

13

On-Site Management of Injuries and Illnesses

Employees become injured or ill at work at least as frequently as they do when not at work. Some of these sicknesses may be general in nature, such as the flu or diabetes. Some may be work-related, such as trauma from an accident or a chemical overexposure. Other incidents may need further investigation to determine whether they are work-related or not, such as a sudden loss of consciousness or a severe headache. The supervisor's immediate concern is not to determine compensability but to ensure the provision of proper medical attention to the stricken employee.

Ensuring Preparedness

Given that employees will become incapacitated during working hours, managers must plan proper on-site responses, depending on the type and severity of the illness or injury. A first step is designating preferred medical providers for every possible contingency, from minor injuries to life-threatening events, as discussed in Chapter 12. The manager should post the names, addresses, and telephone numbers of these providers in locations easily accessible to employees in an emergency.

Establishing a Plan and Written Protocol

Responding correctly and promptly can reduce the severity of many injuries and illnesses. For example, obtaining rapid treatment for an employee with a foreign body in the eye will often prevent permanent damage.

Managers must establish a written protocol for handling injuries and illnesses over all normal working hours, especially if those include 24-hour, 7-days-a-week operations. A major failing of many injured employee response plans (IERPs) is that they cover only "best case" scenarios and don't apply to late-night, weekend, or off-premises accidents, when staffing is likely to be lower and many health-care facilities are closed or at a considerable distance. Make sure the plan is applicable anytime, anywhere.

The **Injured-Employee Response Plan** (Form 13-1) should specify who the first responders are, to whom the injury or illness should be reported, the scope of on-site first aid, what decision logic is used for referral to an off-site medical facility, and what transportation arrangements are appropriate.

First Responders

The most cost-effective arrangement for larger organizations is to establish a corporate medical department, staffed with a consulting physician and one registered nurse for every 500 employees, particularly in a manufacturing environment. Occupational health nurses are then available on-site to provide immediate care and appropriate referral in the event of an accident. In addition, managers can delegate to the medical department the responsibility for establishing all policies and procedures relating to the medical care of employees.

If an employer does not have a medical department or immediate access to a nearby medical facility, each worksite should appoint and train interested volunteers to serve on its first-aid team. The Red Cross, hospitals, and nurse consultants provide first-aid classes, including cardiopulmonary resuscitation (CPR) and other skills. Training and CPR certification have to be renewed periodically. In addition, those who are expected by employers to respond to emergencies involving potential exposure to body fluids are subject to OSHA's Bloodborne Pathogens Standard and its associated training and vaccination requirements.

Reporting to the Supervisor

The IERP should specify that after the first-aid team has been called, someone should notify the supervisor. The supervisor's role may include the following immediate and subsequent responsibilities:

- Ensuring that first responders have arrived
- Assessing the situation
- Preventing further injuries by securing the area
- Arranging off-site medical care for the injured person

- Securing transportation and accompanying the employee to a health-care facility
- Recording the events surrounding the accident
- Notifying the workers' comp coordinator
- Conducting a preliminary accident investigation
- Making preliminary recommendations for prevention
- Maintaining contact with the injured employee through recovery

Immediate Actions Required and Allowed

The IERP should describe the extent of at-the-scene treatment that the company expects its first responders to provide. Unless the facility has an on-site medical department, most first responders have limited medical skills. The IERP should limit the members of this team to injury assessment, application of any life-saving techniques, determining whether outside medical care is needed and, if so, what type, and communicating with the off-site facility regarding the suspected nature of the injury and any on-site treatment given.

Injury Triage

Triage refers to sorting of the injured or ill according to the level of care they require. During wartime and disasters, the technique may be used to allocate scarce medical resources to those who have the highest probability of surviving. In a hospital emergency department, triage ensures that those with the most serious ailments are given treatment priority. In the work environment, the first-aid team or the supervisor can use triage to determine whether a stricken employee should be taken by ambulance to the hospital or should be referred to a nonemergency medical center, such as a doctor's office. The **Injury/Illness Referral Guide** (Form 13-2) should be readily available to first responders as an aid in injury triage.

> **Example** An employee who was machining aluminum parts began to complain to his co-workers of lightheadedness and nausea. He suddenly lost consciousness and fell to the floor. A co-worker summoned the first-aid team, whose members smelled a pungent odor in the area and surmised that solvent fumes escaping from the degreaser had overwhelmed the employee. Since possibly life-saving treatment was required, they called an ambulance, while removing the affected employee to fresh air. They explained to the ambulance crew the likely scenario and provided a copy of the material safety data sheet (MSDS) for the degreaser solvent suspected of causing the accident.

> **Practical tip** As a general rule, send any employee with a life- or limb-threatening injury or illness to a hospital emergency department by

ambulance. Those with less serious injuries can usually receive adequate medical care and be treated faster at walk-in medical centers, clinics, or doctors' offices.

Transportation

Assessment of the type and severity of the injury also determines the method of transportation. Although it may seem quickest to transport a severely injured employee by private car, doing so may endanger both the transporting and the injured employee. The employee's condition may deteriorate on the way, and the driver may be unequipped to help or at personal risk from a confused or agitated passenger.

The IERP should clearly spell out under what circumstances a co-worker may transport an injured employee, when an employee can be advised to go alone, and when an ambulance is required. Avoid rigid policies that invite rule breaking.

> **Example** A manufacturer established a rule that all injured or ill employees had to be transported by ambulance, regardless of severity of the condition. Thus, ambulances were summoned for those with splinters, small particles in the eye, and other minor trauma. Soon, employees stopped reporting small injuries and supervisors began to break the rule by providing transportation. Management should have offered written guidance and training on appropriate means of transportation, based on the nature of the injury.

Training Supervisors and the First-Aid Team

Training supervisors and the first-aid team in accident management is as important as locating proper medical care and planning emergency responses. The safety committee should provide training periodically as part of its general disaster-preparedness activities. Just as a well-run facility has fire, chemical-spill, and other disaster drills, so too should there be accident-response drills on all shifts.

The safety committee should write up several scenarios and ask supervisors and the first-aid team to respond to simulated accident scenes that are realistic for the setting, from catastrophic to seemingly minor. The committee can observe the drill and make suggestions for improved responses.

> **Example** The safety committee at a fabric-finishing company staged an accident scenario of an employee caught in a rolling mill late at night. The supervisor had to locate maintenance workers to free the "trapped" employee, while the first-aid team devised ways to monitor the employee's condition. Another employee simulated calling an ambulance. As a result of this drill, the safety committee determined that more maintenance workers were needed at night,

either on an on-call or permanent basis, in the event that an actual entrapment occurred.

The training should include familiarizing supervisors and others with the state's workers' comp laws governing an employee's choice of medical provider, all company-specific policies, an employee's right to refuse treatment, and the psychology of illness. A person who has suffered an injury often does not make good decisions and needs help to choose appropriately. Although no one can be coerced into accepting medical treatment, the supervisor or the first-aid team should try persuasion, particularly for head injuries.

> **Example** A maintenance worker at a machine shop straightened up suddenly and struck the back of his head on a protruding metal bar. The impact made a loud noise, but the employee refused all offers of off-site medical care and returned to his duties. The next day, however, he complained of double vision, dizziness, and headache. He was taken to the hospital, where he received life-saving treatment for a subdural hematoma (blood clot on the brain).

If an injured employee continues to refuse medical care, call the company's medical department or designated medical provider for advice. If the injured employee's performance is impaired, but the employee refuses care, the supervisor should consult with a superior about the next step. If the employee is sent home as a result of impaired performance and refusal of care, provide transportation, notify a family member, and call frequently to check on the employee's condition.

Sources of Further Information

DiBenedetto DV, Harris JS, McCunney RJ. *The OEM Occupational Health and Safety Manual.* Beverly, MA, OEM Press, 1992 (with 1993 update).

Weeks JL, Levy BS, Wagner GR. *Preventing Occupational Disease and Injury.* Washington, DC, American Public Health Association, 1991.

Workers' Compensation Board of British Columbia. *Industrial First Aid: A Training Manual.* New York, Van Nostrand Reinhold, 1991.

Form 13-1, Injured-Employee Response Plan

Purpose of the Form

- To clarify roles for supervisor and first-aid team in an accident
- To ensure advance planning for accident response in less-than-ideal situations

Use of the Form

- Distribute the plan to all supervisors and first-aid members.
- Review and revise it annually.

Form 13-1

INJURED-EMPLOYEE RESPONSE PLAN

1. In the event that an employee becomes injured or ill at work (other than minor injuries), the supervisor should summon the first-aid team. Do not leave the injured employee unattended unless there is no alternative.

2. The first-aid team should assess the employee's condition and provide appropriate stabilizing treatment. As a result of the assessment, the first-aid team makes the recommendation about the need for off-site medical treatment and the level of care (hospital, clinic, physician's office), based on the Injury/Illness Referral Guide (Form 13-2).

3. If the employee has a life- or limb-threatening injury or illness, the first-aid team should call an ambulance. If the employee has a less serious illness or injury, the supervisor may elect to drive the employee to the designated medical provider or ask the employee to provide his or her own transportation.

4. The supervisor should function as the accident-site coordinator, ensuring that the first-aid team responds in a timely manner, obtaining other personnel and supplies as needed, communicating messages as requested, securing the site to prevent further injuries or damage, and noting accident details for later recording. If there is an inadequate number of personnel on duty to assist, the supervisor should activate the disaster plan's employee call-up system.

5. If the injured employee is sent off site, the first-aid team should send with the employee a brief written assessment of the employee's condition and any treatment rendered. In the event that a chemical exposure is likely, the team should send the proper material safety data sheets (MSDSs).

6. If the employee refuses medical care for an injury or illness that appears potentially serious, the supervisor and the first-aid team should try to persuade the employee otherwise. If the employee still refuses care, the supervisor should notify the division manager and document the refusal on the Supervisor's Report of Employee Accident (Form 14-1).

Workers' Comp Management from A to Z: A "How to" Guide with Forms. © Nancy Nivison Menzel, OEM Press, Beverly, MA, 1994.

Form 13-2, Injury/Illness Referral Guide

Purpose of the Form

- To clarify types of injuries needing ambulance and emergency care
- To provide names, addresses, and telephone numbers of health-care providers and ambulances

Use of the Form

- Post the guide in every department.
- Review it for accuracy every 6 months.

Form 13-2

INJURY/ILLNESS REFERRAL GUIDE

Employees hurt at work may need medical care beyond first aid, depending on the type or severity of the injury or illness. In some instances, the employee may state that the accident has not produced any injury and refuse care. However, in all cases of blows to the head or acute trauma, supervisors should nevertheless urge same-day medical attention. If off-site medical care is needed, use the guide below to decide the type of facility.

MAJOR INJURIES/ILLNESSES
Employees with the following injuries or illnesses should be transported (by ambulance, in most cases) to the nearest hospital emergency department:
- Chest pain
- Difficulty breathing
- Loss of, or change in, level of consciousness
- Severe burns
- Head or neck injury
- Penetrating wound of chest or abdomen
- Amputation
- Allergic reaction with tightness in throat, difficulty breathing, or dizziness
- Severe bleeding
- Obvious fracture with deformity
- Falls of greater than 4 feet
- Penetrating eye injuries
- Toxic chemical exposures (swallowing, inhalation, skin contact); send MSDS
- Multiple injuries
- Psychiatric disturbances (hallucinations, delusions)
- Seizure
- Lacerations (cuts) exceeding 2 inches in length

If in doubt about what to do, send the employee to a hospital emergency department.

MINOR INJURIES/ILLNESSES
Employees with the following injuries or illnesses may be driven by the supervisor to the designated medical provider or walk-in center noted below for treatment:
- Minor lacerations (under 2 inches in length) that may need suturing
- Limb injuries without deformity
- Minor eye injuries (flush chemicals from eyes prior to transport)
- Back pain (except if caused by fall of more than 4 feet or unable to walk)
- Skin disorders (rashes, ulcerations, minor burns, reddening, pigment change, thickening, growths, abrasions)

AMBULANCE   TELEPHONE

EMERGENCY DEPARTMENT   TELEPHONE   ADDRESS

DESIGNATED MEDICAL PROVIDER   TELEPHONE   ADDRESS

14

Reporting and Investigating Accidents and Incidents

Based on the assumption that *all* accidents are preventable, a logical beginning for an effective safety program is identifying the cause of accidents that *have* occurred or *could have* occurred, then taking steps to prevent the same sequence of events from recurring. Combined with information from the hazard evaluation (Chapter 5), assessment of accident frequency, severity, and causation will provide the safety committee with enough information to rank hazards for urgency of correction.

> **Example** A hazard evaluation noted several unsafe chemical-storage containers, but in the last 10 years, there had been no resulting accidents. However, there had been numerous back injuries associated with transporting the chemicals from the storage to the processing area. Hence, the safety committee gave work-flow problems more immediate attention than chemical storage.

What Is an Accident?

An *accident* is an untoward event that results in personal injury or illness, interruption of production, or property loss.

> **Example** A maintenance employee enters an industrial dryer to inspect the drum without locking it out. A co-worker starts the equipment, trapping the maintenance worker inside and killing him.

> **Example** An employee selects the wrong button for batch feeding chemicals into a mixing tank. The resultant compound is useless and adheres to the sides of the tank, causing the plant to lose production for 5 days, throw out the

chemicals, and devote time to cleaning the mixing tank. No personal injuries occur, however.

What Is an Incident?

An *incident* is the term often used for a so-called "near miss" (more correctly a "near hit") or close call that could have caused an accident but didn't. Incidents are sometimes referred to as safety concerns to differentiate between losses that actually occurred and situations that could have caused loss.

Example Employees of an electric utility complain to the safety committee that one of the supervisors is unable to climb poles due to a knee injury and would be unable to rescue someone in the event of an accident. The disabled supervisor is replaced with an employee who can meet the essential physical requirements of the job.

Companies can prevent many accidents by investigating safety concerns (incidents) as well as accidents. Employees become active participants in creating a safe work environment if they are asked to submit concerns to the safety committee.

What Causes Accidents — People or Things?

Although the overwhelming majority of accidents are caused by people acting unsafely, many companies spend most of their resources to remedy unsafe conditions because it is easier to identify and remedy "things" than to change behavior, although safety professionals are now reporting progress using behavior-modification techniques. The safety committee must use a balanced approach and analyze accident causation for both unsafe acts and unsafe conditions, then develop approaches to control them.

Unsafe Conditions

The safety committee should take steps to inspect the premises for hazards, as described in Chapter 5. Once this is done, investigation of accidents that have occurred may turn up additional unsafe conditions that should be added to the inspection and improvement list.

Unsafe Acts

Most workplace accidents are caused by human error—that is, the employee did something unsafe due to lack of training, poor attention, failure to obey safety rules, management failure, or even intention, among many "human

Workers' Comp Management from A to Z

factors." If the accident resulted from an unsafe act, a thorough investigation will pinpoint the cause and point to the solution.

> **Example** A delivery van double-parked outside a store because the loading zone was blocked with cars. As the driver guided a heavy rack of clothing down the truck's ramp, he stepped into the path of a passing car and was hit. Although it would appear that traffic was the unsafe condition, the immediate cause was an unsafe act—double parking, despite company rules prohibiting this. A contributing factor was that management expected the delivery drivers to adhere to a strict schedule or lose their bonus, which put economic pressure on the drivers to disobey safety rules. Possible solutions include (1) having store managers block loading zones with orange cones on delivery days and (2) lifting economic sanctions for slow deliveries.

Basics of Accident Reporting and Investigation

After initial recording of an accident, another person or group should review the circumstances surrounding the event. The usual procedure is for the supervisor to forward a completed accident report to the safety committee and the workers' comp coordinator (WCC) for analysis. People who are directly involved in (and possibly responsible for) an accident may not be objective. Keep responsibility for immediate accident management with the supervisor but give expanded accident-investigation responsibility to the safety committee.

1. Gathering Information

- The supervisor should provide the safety committee and WCC with a written description of the accident (see Form 14-1, **Supervisor's Report of Employee Accident**), including an assessment of causation and corrective actions taken or recommended.
- If possible, the supervisor should obtain statements from witnesses about the accident.
- The supervisor should record the employee's description of the accident. For example, "Wanda states: 'I fell down the outside stairs when I caught my heel on the rubber mat.'"
- The supervisor should ask the employee how the accident could have been prevented and include his or her suggestions on Form 14-1.
- The safety committee should inspect the accident site to look for obvious hazards and identify possible solutions.

- Either the supervisor or the safety committee should consider taking photographs of the accident scene for later use in accident analysis or for use in a lawsuit.
- The safety committee should interview the supervisor, injured employee, and witnesses, particularly when the recorded accident descriptions differ, depending on the source.

2. Analyzing Information

The safety committee should regularly review accidents and safety concerns to determine whether the cause is an unsafe act, unsafe condition, or a combination of factors. The committee should consider what other causes may have contributed to the accident, such as economic incentives to work at an unsafe pace, labor unrest, threatened layoffs, high turnover rates, or inadequate training, among others.

3. Making Recommendations

Once there is consensus on cause, the safety committee should make written suggestions for corrective action and assign closure dates for accomplishing the changes. The committee should send its recommendations to the supervisor involved, as well as to the person or department responsible for making the changes.

4. Follow-up

The safety committee should ask for progress reports from the supervisor and any others responsible for achieving recommended corrective actions, should track closure dates (see Form 14-2, **Accident Investigation Log**), and should advise senior management if acceptable progress is not made.

> **Example** A stockroom employee suffered back strain after removing a heavy item from a high shelf. The safety committee inspected the premises and found large, bulky objects stored on shelves 6 to 7 feet off the ground. Smaller items were stored at waist level or below. The committee recommended to the supervisor that additional shelves be built at waist level and heavy objects moved to them within 30 days. Smaller items could be stored above eye level if rolling ladders were provided to assist in visualization and retrieval. The safety committee did a follow-up evaluation 1 month later, and because the shelves had not been installed, notified the division manager, who intervened.

5. Documenting and Summarizing Investigations

The safety committee should record its findings and recommendations to help determine program success and highlight problem areas. The committee should summarize its follow-up findings for periodic management reports.

Responding to Safety-Concern Reports

Obviously, the safety committee must investigate all accidents that have occurred, but it should pursue as vigorously all safety concerns and close calls. By involving all employees in the effort to prevent accidents, the safety committee extends its effectiveness. However, the committee must respond to all submitted **Safety-Concern Reports** (Form 14-3), so that employees don't feel their efforts have gone to waste. The safety committee should investigate these close calls the same way as accidents but should first solicit the supervisor's help in resolving or clarifying the identified problem.

Source of Further Information

Tompkins NC. *How to Write a Company Safety Manual.* Boston, Standard Publishing, 1993.

Form 14-1, Supervisor's Report of Employee Accident

Purpose of the Form

- To serve as a written record of the preliminary accident investigation
- To record accident facts and witness statements
- To document initial corrective actions

Use of the Form

- The supervisor should complete the report on the day of accident.
- The supervisor should send the form to the workers' comp coordinator and safety committee on the day of accident.
- The safety committee should review the employee's statement about the accident compared to the supervisor's version and subsequently investigate any inconsistencies.

Form 14-1

SUPERVISOR'S REPORT OF EMPLOYEE ACCIDENT

Name of injured/ill employee _____   Employee's worksite _____

Accident date _____   Accident time _____   Accident location _____

Nature of injury/illness (e.g., strain, sprain, fracture, cut, bruise, scratch, dermatitis, multiple injuries, carpal tunnel syndrome, hearing loss, repetitive motion disorder, etc.): _____

Body part injured (e.g., head, ear, eye, face, arm, hand, finger, elbow, shoulder, wrist, back, leg, thigh, ankle, foot, toe, knee, chest). Specify left/right/upper/lower, which finger(s), toe(s):

_____

Injury source (machinery, chemicals, vehicle, stairs, person, etc.): _____

Describe how injury/exposure occurred (Struck by... Fell from... Exposed to...): _____

_____

To whom was injury/illness reported? _____   Date reported: _____

Employee's statement of what occurred:_____

_____

Date reported as work related: _____   If accident was witnessed, complete witness statement.

What actions of the *employee* contributed to this accident? _____

What actions of *other employees* contributed to this accident? _____

What unsafe *physical conditions* contributed to this accident? _____

What *systems* failed? _____

Suggestions for prevention or correction (include any actions already taken): _____

_____

Was the employee sent off-site for medical care?   ☐ Yes   ☐ No

If "yes," the employee was:

    ☐ returned to full duty; no lost time beyond day of injury/illness.

    ☐ returned to temporary modified duty; no lost time beyond day of injury/illness

    ☐ sent home per doctor's order. Expected return to work date: _____

_____   _____
Supervisor's signature   Date

Send a copy of this form to the workers' compensation coordinator and the safety committee.

Workers' Comp Management from A to Z: A "How to" Guide with Forms. © Nancy Nivison Menzel, OEM Press, Beverly, MA, 1994.

Form 14-1, page 1

SUPERVISOR'S REPORT OF EMPLOYEE ACCIDENT, PART II

WITNESS STATEMENT

NAME OF INJURED EMPLOYEE _____ DATE OF ACCIDENT _____

Describe what happened (Witness 1):

_____

_____

_____

_____

_____

_____

_____ _____ _____ _____
Signature   Address   Telephone   Date

Describe what happened (Witness 2):

_____

_____

_____

_____

_____

_____

_____ _____ _____ _____
Signature   Address   Telephone   Date

Workers' Comp Management from A to Z: A "How to" Guide with Forms. © Nancy Nivison Menzel, OEM Press, Beverly, MA, 1994.

Form 14-2, Accident-Investigation Log

Purpose of the Form

- To track accident investigations and results
- To periodically analyze effectiveness of accident investigations

Use of the Form

- The safety committee should enter summary data on each accident.
  - List the type of accident in a commonly used category, such as caught in/under/between, fall on same level, fall to different level, struck by, slip, inhalation, overexertion, unsafe lifting and carrying, and so forth.
- Record the injury source (sometimes called the "agency of accident")—for example, motor vehicle, metal bar, cement floor.
  - List the cause as either an unsafe act, unsafe condition, or both. Unsafe acts could include making safety devices inoperative, using defective equipment, failure to use personal protective equipment, not following directions, and so forth. Unsafe conditions could include poor housekeeping, hazardous arrangement, unsafe construction, and so forth. Note any system failures (e.g., no lockout program in effect, no training for newly hired employees).
  - List any possible contributing factors, such as mandatory overtime, bonus pay for rapid production, newly hired employees, and so forth.
  - The safety committee should follow up on accidents that show recommendations not achieved in specified time.
  - Every 6 months and annually, the safety committee should total the number of accidents and tabulate causes, agencies, location, supervisor, contributing factors, length of time to closure. It should use results to set accident-reduction goals and to target safety programming.

Form 14-2

ACCIDENT-INVESTIGATION LOG

LOCATION	SUPERVISOR	ACCIDENT DATE	ACCIDENT TYPE	INJURY SOURCE	CAUSE	CONTRIBUTING FACTORS	RECOMMENDATIONS	SCHEDULED	DONE

Workers' Comp Management from A to Z: A "How to" Guide with Forms. © Nancy Nivison Menzel, OEM Press, Beverly, MA, 1994.

Form 14-3, Safety-Concern Report

Purpose of the Form

- To involve employees in safety assessment
- To notify supervisors and the safety committee of possible hazards

Use of the Form

- Educate employees that they should first bring safety concerns to the attention of their supervisors.
- If not satisfied with the action taken, employees should submit a signed Safety-Concern Report to the safety committee.
- The safety committee should ask the employee's supervisor to try to resolve the issue within a specified time period and report on progress to the committee on a specified date.
- If the supervisor is unable to resolve the identified problem, the safety committee should seek additional help from management or other resources.

Form 14-3

SAFETY-CONCERN REPORT

Please report to the supervisor any unsafe conditions, work practices, activities, or equipment that could cause injury or illness, property damage, or work-flow interruptions. If you wish to bring the safety concern to the attention of the safety committee, please complete this form and give it to your safety-committee representative.

Date safety concern noted _____

Location _____

Supervisor to whom you reported this safety concern _____

Describe safety concern: _____

_____

_____

_____

Safety concern caused by (describe work practices or conditions): _____

_____

_____

_____

Suggestions for prevention or correction (include any actions already taken to correct the unsafe work practice or condition): _____

_____

_____

_____

Reported by: _____   _____   _____
               Name   Title   Date

- -

Safety committee plan _____

_____

Action taken _____

Date of next review _____

.

15

Administrative Procedures and Reporting Requirements

There are different workers' comp laws in all 50 states, as well as in American Samoa, Guam, Puerto Rico, and the U.S. Virgin Islands. In addition to these state or territorial laws, there are also federal workers' comp laws (Federal Employees' Compensation Act, District of Columbia Workers' Compensation Act, and Longshore and Harbor Workers' Compensation Act). Each law differs in coverage and structure, but all aim to provide injured workers with prompt medical care and income protection, while reducing the need for, and cost of, litigated settlements. In practice, the laws vary in their ability to meet these goals.

Federal health-care reform has considered covering the cost of workers' comp medical care in addition to medical care for non-work-related conditions, to try to head off cost-shifting into the most advantageous plan. However, implementing this so-called 24-hour coverage is complicated by the differing provisions of state laws, such as mandated treatment protocols or limitations on choice of health-care providers. Although some individual states have experimented with combining benefits, 24-hour coverage faces many hurdles before it can be implemented nationally.

Understanding State Legal Provisions

Managers wishing to control their workers' comp costs and losses should purchase and study copies of the law for every state or jurisdiction in which their organization operates. Contact the state or other jurisdiction's workers' comp administrative agency to find out how to obtain a copy of its law (see

Form 15-1, **Directory of Workers' Compensation Administrators**). Although many workers' comp laws cover public employees, some do not. In addition, some laws do not apply unless there is a minimum number of employees (e.g., Arkansas, Georgia, New Mexico, and North Carolina: 3; Florida, Rhode Island, and South Carolina: 4; Alabama, Mississippi, Tennessee, and Virginia: 5). Laws also vary in their coverage of minors.

Most laws are compulsory, requiring employers to accept their provisions. However, a few states' laws are elective, allowing employers to reject the law if they wish, with certain legal consequences.

Ensuring Compliance with State Law

Each workers' comp law specifies what, how, and when work-related injuries and illnesses must be reported. Whatever law applies, managers should determine whether the employer is complying with all its provisions to avoid fines and legal sanctions. (See Form 15-2, **Employer's Report of Accidents.**)

Most workers' comp jurisdictions mandate reporting of workplace injuries and illnesses within a specified time period after occurrence. Because these reporting requirements often differ from jurisdiction to jurisdiction and often differ from OSHA-recording requirements, an employer who must report injuries and illnesses for a number of states may become confused and make errors. Managers with multi-state responsibilities should have either rapid and efficient internal reporting systems or should consider placing the responsibility at the site level.

Example An oil company with operations in Louisiana, Texas, and Oklahoma had centralized all state reporting. Sites notified the corporate office when a workplace injury occurred, whereupon it submitted an Employer's First Report of Injury to the appropriate workers' comp administrative office. This system resulted in several missed filing deadlines, particularly when paperwork from the sites was delayed. The company reduced the number of late filings by switching to a decentralized reporting system, with the sites responsible for sending an additional copy of the Employer's First Report of Injury to the corporate office for advisement.

Reporting to the Insurer

Insurers vary in their requirements for notification of workplace injuries and which injuries must be reported. Managers should set up the procedure for reporting to insurers or third-party administrators, based on their insurer's requirements, and periodically conduct audits to make sure the protocol is followed. Some insurers are now accepting claim reports by telephone, which reduces the delay in sending indemnity checks to injured employees and provides for more timely claims management.

Sources of Further Information

Nackley JV. *Primer on Workers' Compensation* (2nd ed). Washington, DC, Bureau of National Affairs, 1989.

U.S. Chamber of Commerce. *1993 Analysis of Workers' Compensation Laws*. Washington, DC, U.S. Chamber of Commerce, 1993.

Form 15-1, Directory of Workers' Compensation Administrators

Purpose of Form

- To provide addresses for contacting workers' compensation boards in the United States and Canada

Use of Form

- Employers should contact the administrators in the jurisdictions where they do business to find out how to obtain a copy of the most recent workers' compensation law and associated rules and regulations.

Form 15-1

Directory of Workers' Compensation Administrators

Reprinted with permission from the Chamber of Commerce of the United States from the 1993 Edition of *Analysis of Workers' Compensation Laws*. *Analysis of Workers' Compensation Laws* may be ordered by calling 1-800-638-6582.

ALABAMA
Workmen's Compensation Division
Department of Industrial Relations
Industrial Relations Building
Montgomery, Alabama 36131
(205) 242-2868
  Mr. Randy Ritchie, Administrator

ALASKA
Division of Workers' Compensation
Department of Labor
P.O. Box 25512
Juneau, Alaska 99802-5512
(907) 465-2790
  Mr. Paul Arnoldt, Director

Workers' Compensation Board
Same address as Division
  Ms. Nancy Yusera, Commissioner of Labor
  Mr. Thomas Chandler, Member
  Mr. John H. Creed, Member
  Ms. Harriet Lawlor, Member
  Ms. Joanne Rednall, Member
  Mr. David W. Richards, Member
  Mr. Donald R. Scott, Member
  Mr. Darrell F. Smith, Member
  Mr. Joe J. Thomas II, Member
  Mr. Stephen M. Thompson, Member
  Mr. Richard L. Whitbeck, Member

AMERICAN SAMOA
Workmen's Compensation Commission
Office of the Governor
American Samoa Government
Pago, Pago, American Samoa 96799
  Mr. Moaali'itele Tu'ufuli, Commissioner
  Mr. Tasi Mauga, Administrator

ARIZONA
Industrial Commission
800 West Washington
P.O. Box 19070
Phoenix, Arizona 85005-9070
(602) 542-4411
  Mr. Gordon Marshall, Chairman
  Mr. James B. Whitten, Vice Chairman
  Mr. Larry J. Etchechury, Director
  Ms. Elaine C. Adrian, Ombudsman
  Mr. Antonio Dominguez, Member
  Ms. Gay Conrad Kruglick, Member
  Mr. Edward J. Ryle, Member

ARKANSAS
Workers' Compensation Commission
Justice Building
625 Marshall Street
Little Rock, Arkansas 72201
(501) 682-3930
  Mr. James Daniel, Chairman
  Ms. Pat West Humphrey, Commissioner
  Mr. Allyn C. Tatum, Commissioner

CALIFORNIA
Department of Industrial Relations
Division of Workers' Compensation
455 Golden Gate Avenue
Room 5182
San Francisco, California 94102
(415) 703-3731
  Mr. Casey Young, Administrative Director

Workers' Compensation Appeals Board
455 Golden Gate Avenue
Room 2181
San Francisco, California 94102
(415) 703-1700
  Ms. Diana Marshall, Chairperson
  Mr. Richard Gannon, Commissioner
  Ms. Arlene Heath, Commissioner
  Mr. Jacob Margosian, Commissioner
  Mr. John Oda, Commissioner
  Ms. Jane Weigand, Commissioner
  Mr. Dennis Hannigan, Deputy Commissioner
  Mr. Richard Younkin, Deputy Commissioner

COLORADO
Division of Workers' Compensation
1120 Lincoln Street, 12th Floor
Denver, Colorado 80203
(303) 764-4321
  Mr. Kenneth M. Platt, Director
  Ms. Jacquelin A. Holmes, Deputy Director

Industrial Claims Appeals Office
1120 Lincoln Street, 7th Floor
Denver, Colorado 80203
(303) 894-2378
  Mr. David Cain, Member
  Ms. Kathy Dean, Member
  Ms. Dona Halsey, Member
  Ms. Barbara Heckler, Member
  Mr. William Whitacre, Member

CONNECTICUT
Workers' Compensation Commission
1890 Dixwell Avenue
Hamden, Connecticut 06514
(203) 789-7783
  Mr. Jesse Frankl, Chairman
  Mr. John A. Arcudi, Commissioner
  Ms. Roberta D'Oyen, Commissioner
  Mr. Andrew P. Denuzze, Commissioner
  Mr. Donald Doyle, Commissioner
  Mr. Gerald Kolinsky, Commissioner
  Mr. James J. Metro, Commissioner
  Mr. Angelo dos Santos, Commissioner
  Mr. Michael Sherman, Commissioner
  Mr. Darius J. Spain, Commissioner
  Mr. George Waldron, Commissioner
  Mr. Robin W. Waller, Commissioner
  Mr. A. Thomas White, Jr., Commissioner
  Mr. Frank J. Verrilli, Commissioner

DELAWARE
Industrial Accident Board
State Office Building, 6th Floor
820 North French Street
Wilmington, Delaware 19801
(302) 577-2885
  Mr. Warner T. Foraker, Chairman
  Mr. John F. Kirk, Administrator
  Mr. Calvin Boggs, Member
  Mr. Jesse Hastings, Member
  Mr. James P. Robinson, III, Member
  Mrs. Joyce L. Wright, Member

DISTRICT OF COLUMBIA
Department of Employment Services
Office of Workers' Compensation
1200 Upshur Street, NW
Washington, D.C. 20011
(202) 576-6265
  Mr. Charles Green, Associate Director

FLORIDA
Division of Workers' Compensation
Department of Labor and Employment Security
301 Forrest Building
2728 Centerview Drive
Tallahassee, Florida 32399-0680
(904) 488-2548
  Ms. Ann Clayton, Director

GEORGIA
Board of Workers' Compensation
South Tower, Suite 1000
One CNN Center
Atlanta, Georgia 30303-2788
(404) 656-3875
  Mr. George M. Taylor, Executive Director
  Mr. Don L. Knowles, Commissioner
  Ms. M. Yvette Miller, Director

GUAM
Worker's Compensation Commission
Department of Labor
Government of Guam
P.O. Box 9970
Tamuning, Guam 96931-2970
(671) 646-9324
  Mr. Edward A. Guerrero, Director of Labor
    Ex-Officio Commissioner
  Ms. Judy K. Borja, CPA, Member
  Ms. Monessa G. Lujan, Esq., Member
  Mr. Danny A. Orlino, Member
  Mr. Joe A. Rivera, Member
  Mr. Conrad G. Stinson, Member
  Dr. Sinforoso C. Tolentino, MD, Member
  Mr. Christian L. Delfin, Employment Program
    Administrator

HAWAII
Disability Compensation Division
Department of Labor and Industrial Relations
P.O. Box 3769
Honolulu, Hawaii 96812
(808) 548-4131
  Mr. Keith W. Ahue, Director
  Mr. Gary S. Hamada, Disability
    Compensation Division Administrator

Labor and Industrial Relations Appeals Board
888 Mililani Street
Room 400
Honolulu, Hawaii 96813
(808) 548-6465
  Mr. Frank Yap, Chairman
  Mr. Charles Akama, Member
  Ms. Carol K. Yamamoto, Member

IDAHO
Industrial Commission
317 Main Street
Boise, Idaho 83720
(208) 334-6000
  Mr. Herb Carlson, Commissioner
  Mr. Jim Kearns, Commissioner
  Ms. Betty Richardson, Commissioner
  Mr. Gary Stivers, Executive Director

ILLINOIS
Industrial Commission
100 West Randolph Street
Suite 8-200
Chicago, Illinois 60601
(312) 814-6555
  Mr. Robert J. Malooly, Chairman
  Ms. Joann Fratianni, Commissioner
  Mr. Richard M. Gilgis, Commissioner
  Mr. John H. Hallock, Jr., Commissioner
  Mr. Linzey Jones, Commissioner
  Mr. Barry A. Ketter, Commissioner
  Ms. Jacqueline Kinnaman, Commissioner

INDIANA
Worker's Compensation Board
402 West Washington Street
Room W196
Indianapolis, Indiana 46204
(317) 232-3808
  Mr. Rogelio Dominguez, Chairman
  Ms. Janet S. Bell, Member
  Mr. G. Terrance Coriden, Member
  Mr. Willie Harris, Member
  Mr. Richard J. Noel, Member
  Mr. John A. Rader, Member
  Ms. Anne C. Thomas, Member
  Mr. Douglas Meagher, Executive Secretary

IOWA
Division of Industrial Services
Department of Employment Services
1000 E. Grand Avenue
Des Moines, Iowa 50319
(515) 281-5934
  Mr. Byron K. Orton, Commissioner
  Ms. Sharon L. McDonald, Assistant
    Commissioner

KANSAS
Division of Workers' Compensation
Department of Human Resources
800 SW Jackson St., Ste. 600
Topeka, Kansas 66612-1227
(913) 296-4000
  Mr. George Gomez, Director

KENTUCKY
Department of Workers' Claims
Perimeter Park West
1270 Louisville Road, Building C
Frankfort, Kentucky 40601
(502) 564-5550
  Mr. Armand Angelucci, Chairman
  Hon. L.T. Grant, Commissioner
  Mr. Larry Greathouse, Member
  Mr. Walter W. Turner, Member

LOUISIANA
Department of Labor
Office of Workers' Compensation Admin.
P.O. Box 94040
Baton Rouge, Louisiana 70804-9040
(504) 342-7555
  Mr. Alvin J. Walsh, Assistant Secretary

MAINE
Workers' Compensation Commission
Deering Building
State House Station 27
Augusta, Maine 04333
(207) 289-3751
  Mr. Charles Weeks, Chair
  Mr. Lawrence Carr, Board Member
  Ms. Debra Chaloux, Board Member
  Mr. Ronald Guay, Board Member
  Mr. James Mackie, Board Member
  Ms. Susan Pinette, Board Member
  Ms. Cheryl Russell, Board Member
  Mr. Eugene Sanborn, Board Member

MARYLAND
Workers' Compensation Commission
6 North Liberty Street
Baltimore, Maryland 21201
(410) 333-4700
  Mr. Charles J. Krysiak, Chairman
  Mr. Sidney W. Albert, Commissioner
  Mr. L. Douglas Jefferson, Commissioner
  Mr. Jacques Leeds, Commissioner
  Mr. J. Max Millstone, Commissioner
  Mr. Robert S. Redding, Commissioner
  Mr. Stephen Roesenbaum, Commissioner
  Mr. G. Joseph Sills, Jr., Commissioner
  Ms. Carmel J. Snow, Commissioner
  Mr. Richard Teitel, Commissioner

MASSACHUSETTS
Department of Industrial Accidents
600 Washington Street, 7th floor
Boston, Massachusetts 02111
(617) 727-4900
  Mr. James J. Campbell, Commission
  Hon. Joseph W. Jennings, III, Senior Judge
  Mr. David S. Smith, Deputy Commissioner
  Mr. Stephen M. Linsky, Chief Legal Counsel
  Mr. Thomas J. Griffin, III, Director,
    Division of Administration
  Mr. William D. Sivert, Jr., Deputy Director,
    Division of Administration
  Mr. Douglas W. Sears, Deputy Director,
    Division of Dispute Resolution

MICHIGAN
Bureau of Workers' Disability Compensation
Department of Labor
201 North Washington Square
P.O. Box 30016
Lansing, Michigan 48909
(517) 322-1296
  Mr. Jack F. Wheatley, Director
  Mr. John P. Miron, Chief Deputy Director

Board of Magistrates
201 North Washington Square
P.O. Box 30016
Lansing, Michigan 48909
(517) 335-0642
  Mr. Craig Petersen, Chief Magistrate

Workers' Compensation Appellate Commission
Department of Labor
7150 Harris Drive
P.O. Box 30015
Lansing, Michigan 48909
(517) 335-5828
  Ms. Nancy L. Day, Chairperson
  Mr. Gary Goolsby, Commissioner
  Mr. David A. Neff, Commissioner
  Ms. Sharon L. Smith, Commissioner
  Mr. Jurgen Skoppek, Commissioner
  Ms. Molly Ann Beitner, Commissioner
  Mr. J. Edward Wyszinski, Jr., Commissioner

MINNESOTA
Workers' Compensation Division
Department of Labor and Industry
443 Lafayette Road
St. Paul, Minnesota 55155
(612) 296-6107
  Mr. John B. Lennes, Jr, Commissioner
  Mr. Leo Eide, Assistant Commissioner

Workers' Compensation Court of Appeals
775 Landmark Towers
345 St. Peter Street
St. Paul, Minnesota 55102
(612) 296-6526
  Hon. Steven D. Wheeler, Chief Judge
  Hon. Thomas L. Johnson, Administrator
    Judge
  Hon. Richard C. Hefte, Judge
  Hon. R.V. (Sally) Olsen, Judge
  Hon. Debra A. Wilson, Judge

MISSISSIPPI
Workers' Compensation Commission
1428 Lakeland Drive
P.O. Box 5300
Jackson, Mississippi 39296-5300
(601) 987-4200
  Ms. Claire M. Porter, Chairperson
  Ms. Beverly W. Hogan, Commissioner
  Mr. Mike Nipper, Commissioner
  Mr. Arthur C. Sharpe, Executive Director
  Mrs. Brenda H. Goolsby, Commission
    Secretary

MISSOURI
Division of Workers' Compensation
Department of Labor and Industrial Relations
3315 West Truman Blvd.
P.O. Box 58
Jefferson City, Missouri 65102
(314) 751-4231
  Mr. C. Bruce Cornett, Director
  Mr. Robert A. Crouch, Deputy Director
  Mr. Robert F. Harris, Chief Legal Counsel

Missouri Labor and Industrial Relations
  Commission
3315 West Truman Blvd.
P.O. Box 599
Jefferson City, Missouri 65102
(314) 751-2461
  Ms. Elizabeth Healey, Chairman
  Mr. Philip Barry, Member
  Mr. Tom Deuschle, Member

MONTANA
State Fund Insurance Company
P.O. Box 4759
Helena, Montana 59604-4759
(406) 444-6518
  Mr. Patrick J. Sweeney, President

Workers' Compensation Court
P.O. Box 537
Helena, Montana 59624
(406) 444-7794
  Hon. Timothy W. Reardon, Judge
  Mr. Robert Campbell, Hearings Examiner
  Ms. Clarice Beck, Hearings Examiner

NEBRASKA
Workers' Compensation Court
State House, 12th Floor
P.O. Box 98908
Lincoln, Nebraska 68509-8908
(402) 471-2568
  Hon. Ben Novicoff, Presiding Judge
  Hon. Mark A. Buchholz, Judge
  Hon. Michael P. Cavel, Judge
  Hon. James R. Coe, Judge
  Hon. Paul E. LeClair, Judge
  Hon. James P. Monen, Judge
  Hon. Ted W. Vrana, Judge
  Ms. Carol S. Thompson, Administrator

NEVADA
State Industrial Insurance System
515 East Musser Street
Carson City, Nevada 89714
(702) 687-5284
  Mr. Donald E. Jayne, General Manager

Department of Industrial Relations
1390 South Curry Street
Carson City, Nevada 89710
(702) 687-3032
  Mr. Larry McCracken, Director

NEW HAMPSHIRE
Department of Labor
Division of Workers' Compensation
State Office Park South
95 Pleasant Court
Concord, New Hampshire 03301
(603) 271-3171
  Mr. Richard M. Flynn, Commissioner
  Mr. David M. Wihby, Deputy Commissioner
  Ms. Kathryn Barger, Director, WC Program

NEW JERSEY
Department of Labor
Division of Workers' Compensation
Call Number 381
Trenton, New Jersey 08625-0381
(609) 292-2414
  Hon. Mark E. Litowitz, Chief Judge and
    Director

NEW MEXICO
Workers' Compensation Administration
1820 Randolph Rd, SE
P.O. Box 27198
Albuquerque, New Mexico 87125-7198
(505) 841-6000
  Mr. Gerald B. Stuyvesant, Director
  Mr. Robert J. Horwitz, Deputy Director for
    Operations
  Mr. Kenneth L. Payne, Deputy Director for
    Regulations
  Hon. Pete Dinelli, Judge
  Hon. Gregory Griego, Judge
  Hon. MaryAnn Lunderman, Judge
  Hon. Rosa Q. Valencia, Judge
  Hon. Joseph Wiltgen, Judge

NEW YORK
Workers' Compensation Board
180 Livingston Street
Brooklyn, New York 11248
(718) 802-6666
  Ms. Barbara Patton, Chairwoman
  Mr. Thomas A. Dunne, Vice Chairman
  Mr. Thomas H. Canty, Executive Director
  Mr. Raymond A. Charles, Jr., Member
  Ms. Barbara C. Deinhardt, Member
  Ms. Julia Jorge, Member
  Ms. Lindy Corn Koren, Member
  Mr. Carmine Perrotta, Member
  Mr. Walter Shields, Member
  Ms. Ilene J. Slater, Member
  Mr. Joseph A. Tauriello, Member
  Mr. Ferdinand Tremiti, Member

NORTH CAROLINA
Industrial Commission
Dobbs Building
430 North Salisbury Street
Raleigh, North Carolina 27611
(919) 733-4820
  Mr. James J. Booker, Chairman
  Mr. J. Harold Davis, Commissioner
  Mr. Randolph Ward, Commissioner

NORTH DAKOTA
Workers Compensation Bureau
Russel Building-Hwy. 83 North
4007 N. State Street
Bismarck, North Dakota 58501-0600
(701) 224-3800
  Ms. Diane Alm, Executive Director

Workers Compensation Fund
Same address as Bureau

OHIO
Workers' Compensation Board
30 West Spring Street
Columbus, Ohio 43266-0581
(614) 466-2950
  Mr. Wes Trimble, Administrator
  Mr. Michael J. Knilans, Chairman
  Mr. Joseph Tomasi, Secretary
  Mr. Joseph M. Coyle, Member
  Mr. Donald C. Fanta, Member
  Mr. John R. Hodges, Member
  Mr. Frederick A. Matthews, Member
  Mr. Richard D. Schafstall, Member
  Mr. Joseph Tomasi, Member
  Mr. Paul J. Witte, Member
  Mr. Ross Boggs, Jr., Legislative Member
  Mr. Robert L. Burch, Legislative Member
  Mr. Robert Corbin, Legislative Member
  Mr. Robert C. Cupp, Legislative Member

Industrial Commission
Same address as Bureau
(614) 466-3010
  Mr. Donald M. Colusard, Chairman
  Mr. Robert L. McAllister, Vice-Chairman
  Mr. Richard Geltzer, Member
  Mr. Robert E. Levitt, Member
  Mr. James Mayfield, Member

State Insurance Fund
Same address as Bureau

OKLAHOMA
Oklahoma Workers' Compensation Court
1915 N. Stiles
Oklahoma City, Oklahoma 73105
(405) 557-7600
  Hon. Jerry Salyor, Presiding Judge
  Hon. Louis Buchanan, Judge
  Hon. Ben P. Choate, Jr., Judge
  Hon. Noma D. Gurich, Judge
  Hon. Dick Lynn, Judge
  Hon. Terry A. Pendell, Judge
  Hon. James S. Porter, Judge
  Hon. Kimberly E. West, Judge
  Hon. Ozella M. Willis, Judge

OREGON
Department of Insurance & Finance
21 Labor and Industries Building
Salem, Oregon 97310
(503) 378-4100
  Mr. Gary K. Weeks, Director

Workers' Compensation Board
480 Church Street SE
Salem, Oregon 97310
(503) 378-3308
  Ms. Mary Neidig, Acting Chairman
  Mr. Robert Brazeau, Member
  Mr. Tom Gunn, Member
  Mr. Donald Hooton, Member
  Ms. Kay Kinsley, Member
  Mr. Jim Moller, Member
  Mr. Rudolph Westerband, Member
  Mr. Dan Kennedy, Administrator

PENNSYLVANIA
Bureau of Workers' Compensation
Department of Labor and Industry
1171 South Cameron Street, Room 103
Harrisburg, Pennsylvania 17104-2501
(717) 783-5421
  Mr. Carl M. Lorine, Director

Workmen's Compensation Appeal Board
1171 South Cameron Street, Room 305
Harrisburg, Pennsylvania 17104-2511
(717) 783-7838
  Mr. A. Peter Kanjorski, Chairman
  Mr. William J. Atkinson, Commissioner
  Mr. William R. Davis, Commissioner
  Mr. Harold V. Fergus, Commissioner
  Mr. George F. Pott, Jr., Commissioner
  Mr. C. John Urling, Commissioner
  Mr. J. Douglas Wolfe, Commissioner
  Mr. Norman R. Haigh, Secretary
  Mr. David S. Hawkins, Assistant Secretary

PUERTO RICO
Industrial Commissioner's Office
G.P.O. Box 4466
San Juan, Puerto Rico 00936
(809) 783-2028
  Mr. Gilberto M. Chárriez, President
  Mr. Julio Pomales Santiago, Commissioner
  Mr. Jorge Méndez Nieves, Commissioner
  Mr. Ramon Domenech-Maldonado,
    Commissioner
  Mr. Luis Duprey Figueroa, Commissioner

State Insurance Fund of Puerto Rico
G.P.O. Box 5028
San Juan, Puerto Rico 00936
  Mr. Alberto A. Baco', Administrator

RHODE ISLAND
Department of Workers' Compensation
610 Manton Avenue
P.O. Box 3500
Providence, Rhode Island 02909
(401) 272-0700
  Mr. William Tammelleo, Director
  Ms. Debra L. Olsson, Deputy Director

Workers' Compensation Court
1 Dorrance Plaza
Providence, Rhode Island 02903
(401) 277-3097
  Mr. Eugene L. Laferriere, Chief Judge
  Mr. Robert F. Arrigan, Judge
  Mr. William G. Gilroy, Judge
  Mr. Andrew E. McConnell, Judge
  Ms. Constance Messore, Judge
  Mr. Carmine Rao, Judge
  Mr. Dennis Revens, Acting Administrator
  Mr. John Rotondi, Judge

SOUTH CAROLINA
Workers' Compensation Commission
1612 Marion Street
P.O. Box 1715
Columbia, South Carolina 29202
(803) 737-5700
  Mr. Walter Hundley, Chairman
  Mr. Vernon F. Dunbar, Vice Chair
  Mr. William Clyburn, Commissioner
  Mr. David W. Huffstetler, Commissioner
  Mr. Marvin F. Kittrell, Commissioner
  Mr. Thomas M. Marchant, III, Commissioner
  Ms. Sherry Shealy Martschink,
    Commissioner
  Mr. Michael Grant LeFever, Executive
    Director

SOUTH DAKOTA
Division of Labor and Management
Department of Labor
Kneip Building, Third Floor
700 Governors Drive
Pierre, South Dakota 57501-2277
(605) 773-3681
  Mr. W.H. Engberg, Director

TENNESSEE
Workers' Compensation Division
Department of Labor
501 Union Building
Second Floor
Nashville, Tennessee 37243-0661
(615) 741-2395
  Mrs. Sue Ann Head, Director

TEXAS
Workers' Compensation Commission
Southfield Building
4000 South IH 35
Austin, Texas 78704
(512) 448-7900
  Mr. Edward K. Hayse, Jr., Chairman
  Mr. Ramon Class, Commissioner
  Mr. Joe Hanson, Commissioner
  Mr. O.D. Kenemore, Commissioner
  Mr. Dewey Mark, Commissioner
  Mr. Todd Brown, Director

UTAH
Industrial Commission
160 East 300 South
Salt Lake City, Utah 84111
(801) 530-6800
  Mr. Stephen M. Hadley, Chairman
  Mr. Thomas Carlson, Commissioner
  Ms. Colleen Colton, Commissioner

VERMONT
Department of Labor and Industry
National Life Building
Drawer 20
Montpelier, Vermont 05620-3401
(802) 828-2286
  Mr. Charles D. Bond, Director

VIRGIN ISLANDS
Department of Labor
Workers' Compensation Division
2131 Hospital Street
Christiansted, St. Croix,
  Virgin Islands 00820-4666
(809) 773-0471
  Mr. Adelbert Anduze, Director

VIRGINIA
Workers' Compensation Commission
1000 DMV Drive
P.O. Box 1794
Richmond, Virginia 23214
(804) 367-8600
  Mr. Charles G. James, Chairman
  Mr. Charles G. James, Commissioner
  Mr. Robert P. Joyner, Commissioner
  Mr. William E. O'Neill, Commissioner

WASHINGTON
Department of Labor and Industries
Headquarters Building
7273 Linderson Way, SW, 5th Floor
Olympia, Washington 98504
  Mr. Joseph A. Dear, Director
    (206) 956-4200
  Mr. Robert L. McCallister, Deputy Director
    for Industrial Insurance
    (206) 956-4209
  Ms. Dorette Markham, Deputy Director for
    Policy and Planning
    (206) 956-4205

Board of Industrial Insurance Appeals
410 West 5th Street
Capitol Center Building
Mail Stop FN 21
Olympia, Washington 98504
(206) 753-6823
  Ms. Sara T. Harmon, Chairperson
  Mr. Frank E. Fennerty, Jr., Member
  Mr. Phillip T. Bork, Member

WEST VIRGINIA
Bureau of Employment Programs
Workers' Compensation Division
Executive Offices
601 Morris Street
Charleston, West Virginia 25332-1416
(304) 558-0475
  Mr. Andrew Richardson, Commissioner
  Mr. John H. Kozak, Executive Secretary

Workers' Compensation Appeal Board
601 Morris Street, Room 303
Charleston, West Virginia 25301
  Mr. Richard Thompson, Chairman
  Dr. Eli Dragisich, Member
  Mr. R. Joseph Zak, Member

WISCONSIN
Workers' Compensation Division
Department of Industry, Labor, and
  Human Relations
201 East Washington Avenue
Room 161
P.O. Box 7901
Madison, Wisconsin 53707
(608) 266-1340
  Mr. Greg Frigo, Administrator

Labor and Industry Review Commission
P.O. Box 8126
Madison, Wisconsin 53708
(608) 266-9850
  Ms. Pamela Anderson, Chairperson

WYOMING
Workers' Compensation Division
Department of Employment
122 West 25th Street, 2nd Floor
East Wing, Herschler Building
Cheyenne, Wyoming 82002-0700
(307) 777-7159
  Mr. Dennis Guilford, Administrator
    (307) 777-6763 Underwriting Contributors
  Ms. Betty Duagan, Underwriting
    Program Manager
    (307)777-7441—Claims
  Mr. Marty Muellen, Claims Program Manager

Industrial Accident Fund
Same address as Division

UNITED STATES
Department of Labor
Employment Standards Administration
Washington, D.C. 20210
(202) 219-6091
   Mr. John Fraser, Acting Assistant Secretary

Office of Workers' Compensation Programs
(202) 219-7503
   Mr. Lawrence W. Rogers, Jr., Director

Division of Coal Mine Workers' Compensation
(202) 219-6692
   Mr. James DeMarce, Director

Division of Federal Employees' Compensation
(202) 219-7552
   Mr. Thomas M. Markey, Director

Division of Longshore and Harbor Workers'
   Compensation
(202) 219-8572
   Mr. Joseph F. Olimpio, Director

Division of Planning Policy & Standards
(202) 219-7293
   Ms. Diane Svenonius, Director

Benefits Review Board
800 K Street, NW, Suite 500
Washington, D.C. 20001-8001
(202) 633-7500
   Mr. James F. Brown, Adm. Appeals Judge
   Mrs. Nancy S. Dolder, Adm. Appeals Judge
   Mr. Leonard N. Lawrence, Adm. Appeals
      Judge
   Ms. Regina C. McGranery, Adm. Appeals
      Judge
   Mr. Roy B. Smith, Adm. Appeals Judge
   Ms. Betty J. Stage, Adm. Appeals Judge

Employees' Compensation Appeals Board
300 Reporters Building
7th & D Streets, S.W., Room 300
Washington, D.C. 20210
(202) 401-8600
   Mr. Michael J. Walsh, Chairman
   Mr. David S. Gerson, Member
   Mr. George E. Rivers, Member
   Mr. Willie T.C. Thomas, Alternate Member
   Mr. Michael E. Groom, Alternate Member

ALBERTA
Workers' Compensation Board
P.O. Box 2415
9912 107 Street
Edmonton, Alberta T5J 2S5
(403) 498-4000
   Dr. John Cowell, President and Chief
      Executive Officer
   Mr. W.E. (Bill) McDonald, Vice President,
      Employer Affairs
   Mr. Terry L. Murphy, Vice President,
      Claimant & Health Care Services
   Mr. David Renwick, Vice President &
      Chief Financial Officer

BRITISH COLUMBIA
Workers' Compensation Board
P.O. Box 5350
Vancouver, British Columbia V6B 5L5
(604) 273-2266
   Mr. Jim Dorsey, Chairman of the
      Board of Governors
   Mr. Ken Dye, CEO and President
   Mrs. Connie Munro, Chief Appeal
      Commissioner

MANITOBA
Workers' Compensation Board
333 Maryland Street
Winnipeg, Manitoba R3G 1M2
(204) 786-5471
   Mr. Wally Fox-Decent, Chair
   Mr. Thomas Farrell, CEO
   Mr. George Chapman
   Ms. Laverne Cherray
   Ms. Margaret Day
   Mr. Ed Gallos
   Ms. Marla Niekamp
   Mr. Cal Roberts
   Mr. Marvin Seale
   Mr. Allan Smeall
   Mr. Bruno Zimmer

Workers' Compensation Appeals Board
175 Hargrave
Room 311
Winnipeg, Manitoba R3C 3R8
   Mr. George Davis, Chief Appeal
      Commissioner
   Mr. William de Bakker, Appeal Chairperson
   Ms. Clare Baum, Commissioner
   Mr. Rod Frisken, Commissioner

NEW BRUNSWICK
Workers' Compensation Board
1 Portland Street
P.O. Box 160
Saint John, New Brunswick E2L 3X9
(506) 632-2200
   Mr. John Pauchorne, Chairman
   Mr. Leonard Arsenault, Vice Chair
   Mr. Martine Cormier, Board Secretary
   Mr. Brian E. H. Baxter, Executive Director,
      Administration & Finance
   Ms. Nora Kelly, Executive Director,
      Operations
   Ms. M. Dianne Ormandy, Executive Director
      Workers' Rehabilitation Centre
   Mr. Allan Levine, Member
   Mrs. Yvonne Pascon, Member

NEWFOUNDLAND
Workers' Compensation Commission
P.O. Box 9000
Station B
St. John's, Newfoundland A1A 3B8
(709) 778-1000
   Mr. Derek Forsey, Executive Director
      of Corporate Services
   Mr. Norm Kennedy, Executive Director
of Compensation Services
   Ms. Penelope Rowe, Chairperson, Board of
      Directors

NORTHWEST TERRITORIES
Workers' Compensation Board
P.O. Box 8888
Yellowknife, Northwest Territories X1A 2R3
(403) 920-3888
   Mr. Jeffrey Gilmour, Chairman
   Mr. Gerry Meier, General Manager & COO
   Ms. Dorothy Chattell, Manager Finance &
      Administrative Services
   Ms. Margaret Halifax, Manager, Claims &
      Rehabilitation Services
   Mr. Mike Swinarski, Manager,
      Revenue Services

NOVA SCOTIA
Workers' Compensation Board
5668 South Street
P.O. Box 1150
Halifax, Nova Scotia B3J 2Y2
(902) 424-8440
   Dr. Robert Elgie, Chairman
   Mr. David Stuewe, CEO

Workers' Compensation Appeal Board
8th Floor, Lord Nelson Arcade
5675 Spring Garden Road
P.O. Box 3311
Halifax, Nova Scotia B3J 3J1
(902) 424-4014
   Ms. Linda Mambolin, Chairperson
   Mr. Ivo Winter, Vice Chair
   Ms. Marian Ferguson, Vice Chair
   Mr. John J. O'Brien, Executive Officer
   Mr. James Neville, Member
   Mr. Carl Palmer, Member

ONTARIO
Workers' Compensation Board
2 Bloor Street East
Toronto, Ontario M4W 3C3
(416) 927-6968
   Mr. Odoardo Di Santo, Chair
   Mr. Brian King, Vice-Chair of
      Administration
   Mr. Joseph Duffy, Member
   Mr. Maurice Dutrisac, Member
   Mrs. Daphne FitzGerald, Member
   Mr. James V. Goodison, Vice-Chair,
      Board of Directors (Workers)
   Mr. Stephen Mantis, Member
   Mr. Homer Seguin, Member
   Hon. Robert Stanbury, Vice-Chair,
      Board of Directors (Employers)
   Mr. Carmer Sweica, Member
   Mr. Ronald Ellis, Member Ex-officio

PRINCE EDWARD ISLAND
Workers' Compensation Board
60 Belvedere Avenue
P.O. Box 757
Charlottetown, Prince Edward Island C1A 7L7
(902) 368-5680
   Mr. A.B. Wells, Chief Executive Officer
   Mr. Arthur MacDonald, Chairman
   Mr. Art Howard, Vice Chairman
   Mr. Ron McKeigan, Commissioner

QUEBEC
Commission de la Santé et de la Sécurité
   du travail
1199 de Bleury Street
P.O. Box 6056
Station A
Montréal, Québec H3C 4E1
(514) 873-3503
   Mr. Robert Diamant, Chairman and Chief
      Executive Officer
   Mr. Pierre Shedleur, President and Chief
      Operating Officer
   Mr. Pierre Shedleur, Vice-President, Finance
   Mr. Jacques Privé, Vice-President,
      Operations
   Mrs. Lise Langlois, Vice-President,
      Planning & Programs
   Mrs. Lynda Durand, Vice-President, Services
   Mr. Pierre Lafrance, Secretary-General

SASKATCHEWAN
Workers' Compensation Board
1881 Scarth Street, #200
Regina, Saskatchewan S4P 2L8
(306) 787-4370
   Mr. J.A. McLean, Acting Chairman &
      Executive Secretary
   Mr. George Bissett, Member
   Mr. Leonard Larson, Member
   Mr. K.L. Brown, Chief Administrative Officer

YUKON
Workers' Compensation Board
401 Strickland Street
Whitehorse, Yukon Y1A 4N8
(403) 667-5645
   Mr. William Klassen, Chairperson
   Mr. Scott Widmeyer, Alternate Chair
   Mr. Heiko Franke, Member
   Ms. Chris Haddock, Member
   Mr. Arden Meyer, Member
   Ms. Barbara Moyle, Member

CANADA
Labour Canada
Federal Workers' Compensation Service
Ottawa, Ontario K1A 0J2
(613) 997-2281
   Mr. Mike Valiquette, Director

Merchant Seamen Compensation Board
Labour Canada
Ottawa, Ontario K1A 0J2
   Mr. H.P. Hansan, Chairman
   Capt. J.G. Daniels, Vice Chairman
   Dr. H. Sellers, Member
   Mr. Gary Seymour, Secretary

15-2, Employer's Report of Accidents

Purpose of Form

- To provide the employer with information on reporting and record-keeping requirements and penalties by state and territory
- To help avoid penalties for failure to report by setting up correct reporting procedures

Use of Form

- Locate on the chart all jurisdictions in which the employer does business.
- Verify that each location is complying with appropriate reporting requirements.
- Keep the chart current by ordering each yearly update of the U.S. Chamber of Commerce publication in which it appears (see source line on form).

Form 15-2

Employer's Report of Accidents

Reprinted with permission from the Chamber of Commerce of the United States from the 1993 Edition of *Analysis of Workers' Compensation Laws*. *Analysis of Workers' Compensation Laws* may be ordered by calling 1-800-638-6582.

| JURISDICTION | KEEPING OF ACCIDENT RECORDS BY EMPLOYER[1] | REPORTING REQUIREMENTS[1] | | PENALTIES FOR FAILURE TO REPORT | | |
| | | INJURIES COVERED | TIME LIMIT | FINES | | IMPRISONMENT |
				MAXIMUM	MINIMUM	
ALABAMA	Required	Death or disability exceeding 3 days	Within 15 days			
ALASKA	Required	Death or injury or disease or infection	Within 10 days	(*)		
AMERICAN SAMOA	Required	Injury or death	Within 10 days*	$500		
ARIZONA	Not required	All injuries	Within 10 days			Petty offense
ARKANSAS	Required	Injury or death	Within 10 days and as required	100		
CALIFORNIA	Required	Death cases or serious injuries	Immediately*	100	25	
		1 day or more than first aid	As prescribed			
		Occupational diseases or pesticide poisoning	Within 5 days			
COLORADO	Required	Death cases	Immediately	500 per day		
		All injuries causing lost time of 3 days or more*	Within 10 days*			
CONNECTICUT	Required	Disability of 1 day or more	7 days, or as directed	250		
DELAWARE	Required	Death cases or injuries requiring hospitalization	Within 48 hours*	100	25	Up to 120 days
		Other injuries	Within 10 days*			
DISTRICT OF COLUMBIA	Required	All injuries	Within 10 days	1,000		
FLORIDA	Required	Death cases	Within 24 hours*	500		
		All injuries	Within 10 days and as required*			
GEORGIA	Required	All injuries requiring medical or surgical treatment or causing over 7 days' absence	Within 10 days*	200**	20**	
GUAM	Required	Injury or death	Within 10 days*	500**		
HAWAII	Required	Death cases	Within 48 hours	1,000		Up to 90 days
		All injuries	Within 7 working days			
IDAHO	Required	All injuries requiring medical treatment or causing 1 day's absence	As soon as practicable but not later than 10 days after the accident[2]	300		Up to 6 months
ILLINOIS	Required	Death cases or serious injuries	Within 2 working days	500		Petty offense
		Disability of over 3 days	Between 15th and 25th of month			
		Permanent disability	Soon as determinable			
INDIANA	Required	Disability of more than 1 day	Within 7 days*	500		
IOWA	Required	Disability of more than 3 days	Within 4 days	100	100	
KANSAS	Not required	Death cases	Within 28 days	(*)		
		Disability of 1 day or more	Within 28 days			
KENTUCKY	Required	Disability of more than 1 day	Within 7 days[2]	1,000	100	
LOUISIANA	Required*	Lost time over 1 week or death	Within 10 days	100		
MAINE	Required	All injuries requiring physician services or causing loss of day's work*	Within 7 days	100**		
MARYLAND	Not required	Disability of more than 3 days	Within 10 days	50		
MASSACHUSETTS	Required	Disability of more than 5 days	Within 5 work days[2]	100		
MICHIGAN	Required	Death cases, disabilities of 7 days or more, and specific losses	Immediately			
MINNESOTA	Required	Death or serious injury	Within 48 hours	200		
		Disability of 3 days or more	Within 14 days			
MISSISSIPPI	Required	Disability of one day or working shift	Within 10 days	100*		
MISSOURI	Not required	Death or injury	Within 10 days*	500	50	1 week to 1 year
MONTANA	Required	All injuries	Within 6 days	500	200	
NEBRASKA	Required	Death cases*	Within 48 hours*	1,000*.		Up to 6 months
		All injuries	Within 7 days*			
NEVADA	Required	All injuries	Within 6 working days	1,000		
NEW HAMPSHRIE	Required	All injuries involving lost time or medical expense	Within 5 calendar days	2,500		
NEW JERSEY	Required	All injuries*	Immediately	50	10	

[1] Federal Occupational Safety and Health Act of 1970 established uniform requirements and forms to meet its criteria for all businesses affecting interstate commerce to be used for statistical purposes and compliance with the Act. 12 U.S.C. §651.

[2] Supplemental report required after 60 days, or upon termination of disability.

[3] Attending physician also required to make periodic reports to Board.

[4] Supplemental report within 24 hours after returning to work or knowledge that worker is able to return.

Alaska *20% of unpaid amounts due.

Am. Samoa *Employer must also notify Commissioner upon first payment and suspension of payment, and within 16 days after final payment.

Calif. *To Division of Occupational Safety and Health. Within 5 days of employer's notice or knowledge of employee death, employer must report death to the Department of Industrial Relations.

Colo. *Failure to report tolls time limit for claims. Disability of less than 3 days must be reported to insurer.

Del. *Supplemental report due on termination of disability.

Fla. *Report to carrier within 7 days; if injury caused employee to lose 7 or more days. Supplemental report within 30 days after final payment.

Ga. *Supplemental report on first payment and suspension of payment, and within 30 days after final payment.
**For each refusal or willful neglect to report.

Guam *Failure to report tolls limits for claims.
**For each refusal or willful neglect to report.

Ind. *Supplemental report within 10 days after termination of compensation period.

Kan. *Failure to report tolls time limit for claims. *Childress v. Childress Painting Co.* 1979.

La. *Employers with more than 10 employees must also report within 90 days after death, any nonfatal occupational illness, or injury causing loss of consciousness, restriction of work or motion, job transfer, or medical treatment other than first aid. Violation of confidentiality of any record subject to $500 fine.

Maine *Must report asbestosis, mesothelioma, silicosis, and exposure to heavy metals no later than 30 days from date of diagnosis.
**For each violation. Up to $1,000 for individual and $10,000 for corporation for any willful violation of Act, fraud, or intentional misrepresentation.

Miss. *Added to compensation.

Mo. *Supplemental report within 1 month after original notice to Division.

Neb. *Report may be made by insurance carrier or employer. Failure to report tolls time limits.

N.J. *Uninsured employers are required to report compensable injuries only. If insured, carrier is also required to make report.

| JURISDICTION | KEEPING OF ACCIDENT RECORDS BY EMPLOYER[1] | REPORTING REQUIREMENTS[1] | | PENALTIES FOR FAILURE TO REPORT | | |
| | | INJURIES COVERED | TIME LIMIT | FINES | | |
				MAXIMUM	MINIMUM	IMPRISONMENT
NEW MEXICO	Required	Compensable injuries	Within 10 days	$1,000		
NEW YORK	Required*	Disability of 1 day or more or requiring medical care beyond two first aid treatments	Within 10 days	2,500		Up to 1 year
NORTH CAROLINA	Required	Disability of more than 1 day	Within 5 days[2]	25	5	
NORTH DAKOTA	Not required	No statutory provision				
OHIO	Required	Injuries causing 7 days total disability or more	Within 1 week	250		Up to 30 days
OKLAHOMA	Required	All injuries causing lost time or requiring treatment away from worksite	Within 10 days or a reasonable time	500		
OREGON	Required	All compensable injuries	Within 5 days*	(**)		
PENNSYLVANIA	Required	Death cases	Within 48 hours	100*		Up to 30 days
		Disability of 1 day or more	After 7 days but not later than 10 days			
PUERTO RICO	Required	All injuries	Within 5 days	100		
RHODE ISLAND	Not required	Death cases	Within 48 hours	250		
		Disability of 3 days or more	Within 10 days*			
		Any claim resulting in medical expense	Within 3 years of injury			
SOUTH CAROLINA	Required	All injuries requiring medical attention	Within 10 days[2]	100	10	
SOUTH DAKOTA	Required	(*)	Within 10 days	100		Or 30 days
TENNESSEE	Not required	All injuries requiring medical attention	Within 14 days	100	50	
TEXAS	Required	Disability of more than 1 day; or occupational disease	Within 8 days[2]	500		
UTAH	Required	All injuries requiring medical treatment	Within 1 week	500		
VERMONT	Required	Disability of 1 day or more or requiring medical care	Within 72 hours[2]	25		
VIRGIN ISLANDS	Required	Injury or disease	Within 8 days	500		Up to 6 months
VIRGINIA	Required	All injuries	Within 10 days[2]	250		
WASHINGTON	Not required*	All injuries requiring medical attention	Immediately	250 per offense		
WEST VIRGINIA	Not required	All injuries	Within 5 days			
WISCONSIN	Required	Disability beyond 3-day waiting period	Within 4 days	(*)		
WYOMING	Required	Compensable injuries	Within 10 days	750		Up to 6 months, or both
F.E.C.A.	No provision	Death or probable disability	Immediately			
LONGSHORE ACT	Required	All accidents	10 days	10,000		
ALBERTA	Required	Disability of 1 day or more or requiring medical aid not covered by Alberta Health Care Insurance.	72 hours [3,4]	500	100 per day	
BRITISH COLUMBIA	Required	Death cases	Immediately	(*)		
		All injuries	3 days[3]			
MANITOBA	No provision	All injuries	5 business days	5,000 plus penalty of 150	50	
NEW BRUNSWICK	No provision	All injuries that disable or require medical aid.	3 days[3,4]	50		
NEWFOUNDLAND	No provision	All accidents that disable or require medical aid.	3 days	500*		Up to 3 months, or both.
NORTHWEST TERRITORIES	No provision	All accidents and deaths.	3 days[3,*]	250		
NOVA SCOTIA	No provision	All accidents that disable or require medical aid	3 days[3]	50 for each contravention		
ONTARIO	Required	All accidents that disable or require medical aid	3 days[3,4]	250*		
PRINCE EDWARD ISLAND	No provision	All accidents that disable or require medical aid	3 days	100	10 per day	
QUEBEC	Required, including no loss time injuries	All accidents that caused the worker to be unable to carry on his employment beyond the day on which the employment injury appeared, and those that require medical aid	2 days after day of return to work within first 14 days. If more than 14 days, 2 days after the 14th day.	2,000	500	
SASKATCHEWAN	No provision	All injuries	5 days[3]	500*		
YUKON TERRITORY	No provision	All accidents in which workman is injured	3 days	500		Failure to pay penalty, imprisonment of 6 months to 1 year in aggregate.
CANADIAN MERCHANT SEAMEN'S ACT	No provision	All accidents that disable or require medical aid	60 days	500		Up to 12 months

N.Y. *Also required to provide written statement of right under Act to injured employee or dependent, if deceased.

Ore. *Insurers to send disabling claims to WC Division within 21 days of employer knowledge.
**Quarterly penalty for insurers in excess of 10% of claims reported. Employers liable for civil penalty if induce workers not to report accidents.

Pa. *Late filing of an accident report may also result in the imposition of civil penalties of up to 20% of the compensation awarded and interest accrued and payable.

R.I. *Supplemental report upon termination of disability.

S.D. *Any injury requiring treatment other than first aid or which incapacitates employee for at least 7 calendar days.

Wash. *Not required, but keeping accident records satisfies OSHA requirements.

Wis. *10% of first payment to injured employee. $10 to $100 penalty to state.

B.C. *Employer may be liable for up to full cost of claim.

Man. *Plus 50% of compensation payable.

Nfld. *The cost of the compensation paid for the injury is charged against the employer's experience plus $50 assessment. On summary conviction, the fine is $500 or imprisonment up to 3 months, or both. Claim may be charged against employer's experience for failure to notify.

N.W.T. *Supplemental report within 3 days after return to work or knowledge that worker is able to return.

Ont. *Employer may also be liable for additional fine up to $25,000, on conviction, payable to court.

Sask. *Plus percentage of assessment.

Form 15-2, page 2

16

Obtaining Information on Medical Treatment and Work Restrictions

Once an employee has been injured at work, it is important for planning purposes to learn the recommended treatment plan and the return-to-work schedule. However, obtaining this information in a timely manner is often difficult. One solution is to set up a process to facilitate the smooth flow of information between the health-care provider and the employer.

Legal Considerations

Medical records are protected by confidentiality laws that prohibit others from reviewing them unless the individual expressly gives them access, usually by signing a written release. However, most workers' comp laws allow the insurer to deny payment for a claim unless it can review the medical record relating to that injury or illness.

The employer generally does not have the same right (stated or implied) to review the medical record as the insurer does. However, the employer can ask an injured or ill employee to release medical information following a work-related injury or illness. The best way to accomplish this is by using a form that incorporates a written consent for releasing this information (see Form 16-1, **Employee Consent for Release of Medical Information to Employer**). Employers should review this form with all employees making clear that the purpose of the form is to obtain medical information necessary to plan a reasonable return-to-work schedule and to ensure adequate medical care in the event of injury or illness on the job.

The employee does have the right to refuse to sign the release. If the employee refuses to permit the release of medical information, it is unlikely that the health-care provider will provide the employer with anything other than work status. In these cases, the employer may be able to obtain limited additional information from the insurer to assist in long-term return-to-work planning.

Rationale for, and Scope of, Information Needed

Informed consent means that employees must be told of the extent of information to be released, its uses, and the possible consequences of those uses. One use for post-accident medical information is to allow employers to schedule employees to meet business demands. Receiving information about work status and length of recovery allows the employer to plan for an injured employee's return to work, any activity restrictions that will be involved, and the treatment schedules that will have to be accommodated. The employer also needs to know the severity of the injury/illness for accident investigation and prevention purposes.

However, employees should be informed that if they do sign a general consent, the health-care provider may release information about evidence of drug or alcohol use at the time of the examination, which may adversely affect their employment. This possible consequence may prevent some employees from signing a release. (If the employer has in place a mandatory post-accident drug- and alcohol-testing policy, taking such tests is a condition of continued employment and the results are not subject to the same right of privacy.)

The employer does not need to know, and should not be informed about, conditions unrelated to the specific workplace injury in question, such as human immunodeficiency virus (HIV) status or the presence of degenerative diseases. Therefore, the signed release should limit the information to that associated with a specific work-related injury or illness. In addition, the employer should restrict access to the information only to designated individuals, such as the nurse or physician.

Because there are possible legal ramifications from the employer's obtaining and using this information, the employer should have a lawyer review the wording of the employee-consent form. Make sure that the release is translated into the native languages of all employees.

Obtaining Medical Information

Information on treatment and restrictions should be specific and timely. If an employee with back pain leaves the workplace to receive medical care and later calls in to state only that he or she has been put on bed rest for a week by a doctor in the emergency department, the employer is left in the dark. What was the diagnosis? Is bed rest the appropriate treatment? Who, exactly, was the treating doctor? What is the projected return-to-work date? Is the employee so incapacitated that bed rest is required? Does she need transportation assistance?

> **Practical tip** It's tough to get answers to these questions once the employee has gone home directly after treatment. If the employer calls the injured employee at home, the result is likely to be an endless busy signal, an answering machine screening calls, or a relative responding that the employee is asleep. Avoid these frustrations and disturbances to the employee by establishing a same-day communication protocol, except in cases of hospitalization.

Medical-Treatment Reporting Protocol

Establish a policy requiring employees who have been injured on the job to take with them to the health-care provider a copy of the company's **Medical Treatment Report** (Form 16-2). The employee's consent allowing the release of medical information to the employer (Form 16-1) is incorporated into the Medical Treatment Report. An injured or ill employee should be instructed to give the form to the health-care provider for same-day completion. If the form is short enough, most providers will fill it out if asked.

At the conclusion of the visit to the health-care provider, an injured or ill employee should return to the employer with the completed Medical Treatment Report and give it to a designated individual, such as a supervisor, or a department, such as the human resources department. At this point, the supervisor can review work restrictions and begin to plan for modified work, if required.

Requiring in-person delivery of the form (except in severe cases) allows the supervisor to assess the employee's condition relative to the medical findings noted on the form. Is the employee satisfied with the care he or she received? Does the medical treatment appear to be appropriate or is further referral needed? In-person delivery of current information also reduces the employee's opportunity to exaggerate symptoms or treatment, which is possible over the telephone.

Example An office employee tripped on a loose rug and hit her head on a doorway. She refused medical care on the day of the accident but called in the next day to say she was suffering headaches and blurred vision. She reported that her physician had advised her to stay home for a few days until her symptoms improved. Concerned that the employee was not receiving appropriate medical care in light of her neurologic symptoms, the workers' comp coordinator (WCC) called the employee back. When the WCC asked for the name of the physician, the employee revealed that she had not been examined and that her symptoms weren't "really that bad." The WCC stated that company policy required medical examination for all workers' comp claims and subsequent completion and submission of a Medical Treatment Report. The employee then stated that she was no longer attributing her absence to the accident but was taking a regular sick day instead. The WCC called again later in the day to verify that she was still feeling well and was no longer at risk.

Reviewing the Diagnosis and Treatment

The WCC should review the completed Medical Treatment Report to see whether the diagnosis is a likely result of the accident. In addition, the treatment should be logically associated with the diagnosis. If the diagnosis or treatment seems inappropriate, the WCC should call the health-care provider and ask for a more detailed explanation.

Example An employee of a human services organization was assaulted by a client and suffered minor trauma. She was treated at an occupational health clinic for bruises and contusions. The Medical Treatment Report also indicated that she was treated for possible exposure to bloodborne pathogens. The WCC called the clinic to find out why treatment exceeded the scope of the reported injury and learned that the employee had large areas of chapped skin on her arms that possibly had come in contact with blood or other body fluids from her attacker during the assault. Hence, the diagnosis was more extensive than trauma alone, and the treatment she received was appropriate.

Reviewing Medical Recommendations

The WCC should review the work status and activity restrictions in light of the diagnosis and treatment on the Medical Treatment Report. If an employee has been ordered to stay out of work, yet the employee's condition does not seem to warrant this decision, the WCC should find out the provider's rationale for the restricted work status and, if appropriate, negotiate with the health-care provider to allow modified duty.

In situations in which the health-care provider continues to prohibit modified duty or orders restrictions beyond that which the employee's condition seems to require, the WCC should ask the provider for the medical reasons behind the work-status decision. Usually, the provider offers satisfactory reasons. However, if the answer is vague, such as "I just feel she shouldn't be working," the WCC should keep pushing for the specific medical reasons behind the decision. The real reason may be a request by the injured or ill employee or the health-care provider's inexperience with, or distrust of, modified-duty programs (sometimes with good reason).

> **Example** A utility worker fell from his truck and fractured his ankle. A physician at a nearby hospital's emergency department set the fracture, applied a cast, and ordered the employee to stay at home for 1 week. The company physician called the emergency department to inquire about the medical reasons prompting the no-work decision, in light of the sedentary jobs the company could provide. Upon receiving assurances from the company physician that the injured employee could elevate his leg for most of the work shift while performing a temporary assignment, the treating physician released the employee for a modified-duty assignment (with specific activity restrictions).

The WCC should request a Medical Treatment Report for every visit to a health-care provider. The WCC should look for signs of progress in recovery. If work restrictions are unchanging or worsening, it's time to question the appropriateness of the diagnosis or the effectiveness of treatment. Encourage the injured or ill employee to seek a second medical opinion by explaining the reasons and suggesting alternative health-care providers.

Educating Supervisors and Employees about Employer's Policy

Employers must educate supervisors and employees about the uses and benefits of the medical treatment form. Once employers have explained their need to obtain information about work restrictions, most employees will accept the system. However, some employees will regularly refuse to sign a release, which is their right and should not be held against them.

Employers should send a copy of the Medical Treatment Report to their designated health-care providers and explain the form's purpose and use as a tool to help return injured employees to work. Assure them that the form has been designed to be simple and easy for them to complete. Periodically call and express appreciation for their cooperation. Review completed forms from time to time to see whether health-care providers frequently avoid answering certain questions, which indicates that the questions may need revision.

Form 16-1, Employee Consent for Release of Medical Information to Employer

Purpose of Form

- To allow review of wording and intended use by company lawyer
- To obtain employee's consent to the release of medical information
- To alert employers that they may need a signed consent to obtain medical information

Use of Form

- Have the organization's lawyer review and approve the form's wording and use.
- Print either the long or short version of the approved consent in the Employee section of the Medical Treatment Report (Form 16-2).
- Familiarize supervisors and employees with the reasons for the form's use.
- Advise supervisors and employees that refusing to sign a release of medical information will have no effect on the provision of medical care.

Form 16-1

EMPLOYEE CONSENT FOR RELEASE OF MEDICAL INFORMATION TO EMPLOYER

These are sample consents that should be reviewed by a lawyer familiar with applicable workers' compensation and other laws prior to adopting either one as company policy for obtaining medical information after a workplace accident. Print the approved text (either long or short version) on the Medical Treatment Report (Form 16-2) that employees take with them to the health-care provider.

Sample Employee Consent (Long Version)

I hereby authorize, and give consent to, any health-care provider, including hospitals, clinics, physicians, dentists, and others, to release to (company name _____) any medical or other health-care-related information that it may request or require concerning any treatment, prognosis, results of drug or alcohol tests, or other information about or related to my injury/illness resulting from an alleged work-related incident on or about (date_____).

I understand that I am not legally obligated to sign this consent. I have also been informed that I may ask any questions I desire regarding this consent. All my questions have been asked and answered to my satisfaction. I understand that all information provided will be used to assist my employer in evaluating my injury/illness and my work status and may affect my employment.

_____   _____
Employee's signature   Date

Sample Employee Consent (Short Version)

I give permission to my physicians or other health-care providers, hospitals, or clinics to release the information on this form and, upon request, to release my medical records relating to this injury/illness to my employer. I understand that this information will be used to assist my employer in evaluating my injury/illness and my work status and may affect my employment.

_____   _____
Employee's signature   Date

Workers' Comp Management from A to Z: A "How to" Guide with Forms. © Nancy Nivison Menzel, OEM Press, Beverly, MA, 1994.

Form 16-2, Medical Treatment Report

Purpose of the Form

- To obtain immediate information about the health-care provider's diagnosis, treatment or recommended treatment, and evaluation of employee's work status
- To obtain a written statement from the employee about the accident
- To enhance the employee's impression that the employer cares about the employee's medical treatment and is carefully monitoring the case

Use of Form

- The supervisor should complete the top portion authorizing treatment to reduce delays at the health-care provider's facility.
- The supervisor should ask the employee to complete and sign the Employee section.
- The employee should ask the health-care provider to complete the form at the time of the visit.
- The employee should return to the supervisor with a completed form on the day of *each* visit to the health-care provider, including all follow-up visits. Obviously, hospitalized employees are not expected to follow this protocol.

Workers' Comp Management from A to Z

MEDICAL TREATMENT REPORT

TO BE COMPLETED BY SUPERVISOR

Authorized for treatment by: _____ Title : _____

Date: _____ Location: _____ Tel.: _____

TO BE COMPLETED BY EMPLOYEE *(Employee Signature Required)*

Name _____ SS No. _____ Date _____ Tel. _____

Home street address _____ City _____ Zip _____

Date of injury: _____ Date of first treatment_____

I give permission to my physicians or other health care providers, hospitals, or clinics to release the information on this form and, upon request, to release my medical records relating to this injury/illness to my employer. I understand that this information will be used to assist my employer in evaluating my injury/illness and my work status and may affect my employment.

Date _____ Employee's signature _____

TO BE COMPLETED BY HEALTH-CARE PROVIDER

Diagnosis_____

Treatment (including surgery, physical therapy, medications) _____

_____

MEDICAL RECOMMENDATIONS:

Work status: (Please check <u>all</u> appropriate boxes.)

☐ Patient now totally disabled for work.

☐ Patient expected to return to full duty on _____.

☐ Patient has follow-up appointment on _____.

☐ Patient able to work in a modified duty assignment for _____ days with restrictions below:

☐ Lifting abilities: _____ lb for _____ hr/shift.	☐ No reaching above shoulder height.
☐ Pushing/pulling abilities: _____ lb for _____ hr/shift.	☐ No reaching below waist.
☐ Carrying abilities: _____ lb for _____ hr/shift.	☐ No exposure to dust/fumes.
☐ Bending/twisting/stooping abilities: _____ hr/shift.	☐ Dry work only
☐ No repetitive movement of _____.	☐ No operating machinery/vehicles.
☐ Standing/walking abilities: _____ hr/shift or _____ min/hr.	☐ Other:
☐ Sitting abilities: _____ min/hr.	_____
☐ Endurance abilities:_____ hr/shift, _____ days/wk.	_____

_____ _____ _____ _____
Signature of health-care provider   Address   Tel.   Date

HEALTH-CARE PROVIDER: Please return this form to patient on day of visit.

Workers' Comp Management from A to Z: A "How to" Guide with Forms. © Nancy Nivison Menzel, OEM Press, Beverly, MA, 1994.

17

Involving Supervisors in Accident Prevention and Modified-Duty Programs

Supervisors are chosen for their ability to lead, which is typically measured by productivity. Whether it is a head nurse assigning staff to care for patients or a utility foreman supervising a crew repairing downed power lines, the focus is almost always on production. Were all patients cared for adequately in a 24-hour period? Was power restored in a timely manner? With this type of focus, it is understandable that supervisors spend much of their time trying to improve work flow and output.

How do supervisors view safety? Unfortunately, many treat safety as if it slowed down productivity and hindered job completion. Worse, many supervisors behave as if safety were just a slogan—catchy words with little substance.

Changing Supervisors' Negative Attitudes

Without the whole-hearted cooperation of the supervisor, safety improvement, accident management, and modified-duty programs will fail. There are several approaches to changing supervisors' attitudes, including education, management by objectives, and enforcement.

Importance of Management Commitment

The very highest level of management of the company or institution must make safety a top priority and corporate value. Without this support, supervisors will spend less time on safety and more on the behaviors that are rewarded in the corporate culture. One way management shows its support is by allowing supervisors time to provide and attend safety training sessions and by approving budget requests for needed safety improvements.

Educating Supervisors

After management support, the next most important element in accident prevention and management is educating supervisors that working safely is working efficiently. Unsafe work practices are inefficient because they may cause work stoppage, personal injury, or property loss due to accidents or wasted effort.

Example A seasonal employee of a liquor wholesaler piled more cartons onto his hand truck than the allowed number when his supervisor told him to work faster. When he was pushing an overloaded hand truck up a ramp, he was struck by the top carton, which slid off and broke his leg on its way to the ground. By the time the employee was taken to a hospital emergency department and a replacement helper brought in from another site, the delivery truck was delayed 4 hours and the truck driver was forced to sit idly. If the employee had stayed within the safe load limits, the truck would have left on time, the replacement worker could have completed his original assignment, and the injured employee wouldn't have had to endure an extended convalescence.

The safety committee should put on an annual supervisors' training program that reviews past accidents, highlights unsafe (and inefficient) work practices, and totals the associated costs and losses. The safety committee can often "sell" safety by pointing out that supervisors will have more productive employees if they aren't put in harm's way.

Example A nurse consultant conducted a safety walk-through at a man-made materials manufacturer. She asked a group of employees what was the worst job in the plant. Without hesitation, they showed her the task of filling the top-floor hoppers with chemical compounds. This involved a worker having to go to a remote area, open and lift a 50-lb bag of chemicals, climb a ladder with it, and dump the powder into a hopper for use by the lower production floors. Several employees had injured their backs. Several more were concerned about the effect of inhaling the powder. All wanted to avoid this job and constantly argued about whose turn it was. Consequently, the hoppers frequently ran out, causing work interruptions on the production floor. The nurse met with management and pointed out all the costs of this inefficient system, which was then replaced by a mechanical one that eliminated hand filling, with its associated safety risks and production delays.

Actively Involving Supervisors

Once supervisors begin to see that safety is a tool for efficient production, the next step is to involve them in actively ensuring proper work practices and conditions. One approach is to have supervisors read and sign a list of expectations for their participation (see Form 17-1, **Safety Responsibilities of the Supervisor**) in the safety program. Supervisors should be evaluated on the extent to which they met these responsibilities. A simple evaluation index is the number of accidents and resulting lost workdays in the supervisor's area. If accident frequency and severity don't decline, the supervisor is not meeting management objectives.

Outlining Supervisors' Role in Accident Management

Now that the organization has established an injured employee response plan, has designated a health-care provider, has a system for obtaining timely information about the employee's medical treatment, and has a procedure for investigating accidents, it is time to consolidate these steps into a guide for supervisors to follow. Form 17-2, **Accident-Management Protocol**, summarizes these steps.

Involving Supervisors in Modified-Duty Programs

Because supervisors may have difficulty devising modified-duty assignments, their first response is often that there is no work available. Again, management must educate supervisors about the fact that injured workers can contribute to production and that modified duty will often hasten recovery. With guidance, supervisors can learn to develop modified-duty assignments that are valuable to the department.

In settings where supervisory resistance to modified-duty remains, management should consider a system that penalizes the departmental budget of the injured worker's supervisor. This direct financial consequence is often sufficient to elicit cooperation.

> **Example** A hospital instituted a modified-duty program. Several nursing supervisors balked at providing modified-duty assignments, stating that there were no suitable tasks. The workers' comp coordinator (WCC) reassigned some injured nurses to the dietary department, where they assisted with tray preparation and answered the telephone, among other duties. Although working in the dietary department, the nurses continued to have their salaries drawn from the nursing budget. Within 1 month, the nursing supervisors had devised several modified-duty assignments that were suitable for a variety of restrictions and recaptured the productivity of the injured employees.

Importance of Employer/Employee Communication

Supervisors should contact their injured employees if the employee is out of work. The goal is to express genuine concern for the employee's mishap, make real offers to help, and maintain the link between the employee and the workplace. An injured employee is more likely to return if there is warm communication and a welcoming attitude.

Source of Further Information

Today's Supervisor, National Safety Council, 1121 Spring Lake Drive, Itasca, IL 60143-3201. (Sixteen-page periodical published monthly; subscriptions: $23.00/yr for non-members; $18.00/yr for members; bulk rates available for providing copies to all supervisors within an organization. Written in easy-to-understand style, with many practical tips. Call NSC at [708]285-1121 to order.)

Form 17-1, Safety Responsibilities of the Supervisor

Purpose of Form

- To notify supervisors of management's safety expectations
- To commit supervisors to participation in the safety, accident-management, and modified-duty programs

Use of Form

- Discuss with supervisors the purpose of the form and its contents.
- Have supervisors sign the form.
- Put the form in each supervisor's personnel folder.
- Include in each supervisor's performance evaluation an assessment of effectiveness in carrying out safety responsibilities.

Form 17-1

SAFETY RESPONSIBILITIES OF THE SUPERVISOR

The most efficient way to work is safely. Therefore, we expect supervisors to meet the following expectations:

1. Maintain a safe and hazard-free workplace through regular inspections.

2. Train each employee in safe work methods and procedures:

   a. Explain how and why a job function must be performed a certain way.

   b. Demonstrate the proper way to do the job and then have employees practice the technique while under observation.

   c. Coach and correct employees until they can show they have mastered the correct procedure.

   d. Because it may take some time before all workers acquire safe work skill and habits, regular supervision and training are necessary to prevent unsafe performance and to guard against lax attitudes toward safety.

3. Ensure that each employee has available whatever personal safety equipment or protective clothing is required.

4. Help prevent accidents by maintaining employee interest in safety and motivating employees to recognize and respond to potential hazards.

5. Instruct each employee in how to summon first-aid assistance and where fire extinguishers are located. Explain to each employee the procedure to be followed when evacuating the building during emergencies and fires. Provide disaster drills on a regular basis.

6. Ensure that safety instructions, regulations, and posters are displayed in obvious locations throughout the worksite.

7. Complete a Supervisor's Report of Employee Accident (Form 14-1) for all accidents as soon as practical after providing assistance to the employee and securing the site of the accident.

8. Follow up on all accidents and incidents with an investigation to determine cause and make appropriate corrections or suggestions for correction.

Workers' Comp Management from A to Z: A "How to" Guide with Forms. © Nancy Nivison Menzel, OEM Press, Beverly, MA, 1994.

9. Assist in placing employees with work restrictions in suitable modified-duty work assignments.

10. Contact injured employees to maintain communication.

11. Make safety a part of every employee's performance review.

12. Set a good example by personally following all safety rules.

I agree to carry out these responsibilities as a supervisor. I understand that my performance evaluation will include these criteria.

_____   _____
Supervisor's signature   Date

Workers' Comp Management from A to Z: A "How to" Guide with Forms. © Nancy Nivison Menzel, OEM Press, Beverly, MA, 1994.

Form 17-2, Accident-Management Protocol

Purpose of the Form

- To provide guidance to supervisors on the proper procedure to follow in the event of an accident
- To ensure that attention to injured or ill employee supersedes paperwork

Use of the Form

- Post the form in supervisors' offices.
- The safety committee should review the protocol annually and update it as necessary.

Form 17-2

ACCIDENT-MANAGEMENT PROTOCOL

1. If injured/ill employee requires medical care beyond on-site first aid, supervisor refers employee to preferred medical provider (listed on Injury/Illness Referral Guide [Form 13-2]). Supervisor completes top 2 lines of a Medical Treatment Report (MTR) (Form 16-2) and gives it to employee to take to health-care provider.

↓

2. Employee completes Employee Section of the MTR and signs it prior to giving it to health-care provider (physician, nurse practitioner, emergency department, clinic, or chiropractor) to complete at time of *each* visit.

↓

3. Employee returns MTR to supervisor on same day of visit to health-care provider.

↓

4. Whether or not employee needs off-site medical care, supervisor fills out a Supervisor's Report of Employee Accident (Form 14-1) and sends it and MTR (if applicable) to workers' comp coordinator (WCC). Supervisor also sends copy of Supervisor's Report of Employee Accident to safety committee.

↓

5. WCC begins case-management process and complies with regulatory and insurer reporting as needed. WCC coordinates modified-duty or return-to-work date with supervisor, if accident results in lost time or work restrictions.

↓

6. Supervisor provides supportive communication to employee each time new MTR is received.

↓

7. Supervisor gives to WCC all MTRs as they are received.

↓

8. Case-management process continues until employee is back to work and case is closed.

Workers' Comp Management from A to Z: A "How to" Guide with Forms. © Nancy Nivison Menzel, OEM Press, Beverly, MA, 1994.

18

Ensuring Good
Employer/Employee Relations

Communication between the employer and an employee with a work-related injury or illness is often laden with fear and distrust of the other's actions and motives. The employee's feelings may have undertones of anxiety, self-pity, and resentment, and the employer's may be colored by suspicion, frustration, and anger. A battle line may be drawn, with little chance for peace unless hostilities are reduced through greater understanding and cooperation.

Here is what the employee may be thinking when he or she is at home and out of work following an injury.

Injured worker I'm sitting around not doing anything. I've lost control of my life. All I was trying to do was a day's work for a day's pay. They had me lifting heavier boxes than I should have been. Now I'm on comp and can't pay my bills. No one from work calls or visits; I guess they've forgotten me already. My husband is mad at me. I'm in pain. The insurance company doesn't care about me. My hearing has been delayed. The doctor can't predict if I'll ever be 100% again. I don't know if I'll get my old job back. I don't know if I'll ever work again.

Here is what the employer may be thinking as he or she stares at the work schedule, now shy one employee.

Employer I just know she's faking it. No one saw her move that box when she says she hurt her back. She's only using the system to get some paid time off, while I'm struggling to get the work done. Now my workers' comp premiums are going to go through the roof. I never should have hired her. She wasn't that productive anyway. I'm going to fill her position and not let her back. I'll hire an investigator to watch her activities. She's not going to win this one.

Importance of Effective Communication

Clearly both parties have different agendas and are on the way to a "train wreck" without intervention. As a start, both sides need to practice being sensitive to each other's feelings. It's never a losing strategy to treat people with respect and consideration. Offensive treatment will not dissuade those who intend to defraud the system, but it will alienate otherwise honest claimants.

> **Example** The owner of a small business called one of his injured employees after a 3-day absence and said, "I know you're faking it. If you don't show up for work tomorrow, I'm replacing you." The employee felt that if she showed up in response to this threat, then she would be admitting malingering. Thus, her only choice to protect her honor was to get sicker, which is what happened. After 7 months, this employee is still receiving compensation for what began as a relatively minor back strain.

Facilitating Effective Communication

When an employee is out of work and receiving workers' comp benefits, the workers' comp coordinator (WCC) should write down the goals of the communication and then set up a schedule. This should include an immediate telephone call, followed by other calls and letters on a weekly or more frequent basis. The primary goal is to keep the channels of communication open and to be perceived by the employee as a resource, not an adversary. (See Form 18-1, **Guidelines for Communicating with Injured or Ill Employees**.)

> **Practical tip** Keep absent employees on a mailing list to receive newsletters, staff minutes, memos, production schedules, and other offerings, such as photocopies of notices on the bulletin board. Call and ask for comments on these mailings.

Conveying Empathy and Concern

Keep in mind that the injured employee is most likely experiencing fear and anxiety about the future. The WCC should exhibit empathy for the employee's situation. Sympathy is feeling sorry for someone; empathy is experiencing the other's feelings as if they were your own. Empathy is characterized by understanding and sensitivity. The WCC can exhibit empathy by restating the employee's perceived feelings with statements like,

"That accident must have frightened you" or "You must have gone through a lot because of that accident."

It is also important to express the genuine concern of the organization as a whole. "We were all upset when we heard what had happened." But be sure to add optimism. "We're glad you are receiving such good medical care and are on the mend. We're looking forward to your return."

Maintaining Neutrality

Note that the WCC should not ask confrontational questions, such as "When are you coming back to work?" Avoid blame as well. All accidents are caused by some series of events. It doesn't help recovery for the WCC to state, "I hear that Pete told you over and over that if you kept doing that you'd get shocked. But you wouldn't listen!"

If the WCC does refer to the accident, it should be in terms of prevention. "We want to make sure that this never happens again. What suggestions do you have to pass on to the safety committee?" This makes the employee take an active role and move away from the victim mentality.

Establishing Trust

The most important accomplishment of communication between the WCC and the employee is establishing trust. Because of deep suspicions about motives, neither side may trust the other when the WCC initiates the organization's new communication program. However, if the WCC has previously earned a good reputation as an employee advocate, the WCC will be able to establish trust earlier and earlier in subsequent cases.

One way of establishing trust is to be "up front" and honest about the reason for phone calls and the goals of the case-management process. For example, the WCC can state that the company wants to stay in touch because it is concerned about the employee and wants to assist in the recovery process. The WCC can explain that the company follows guidelines for case management that have been shown to help employees achieve rehabilitation.

Although the WCC should play a prominent role, in some cases the employee has established a strong relationship with someone else who may be able to influence the employee more. This could be a supervisor or mentor, someone the employee respects. If such a relationship exists, consider shifting the communication responsibility to that person. Again, the goal is keeping the lines of communication open.

Sometimes it is useful to establish bonding through the "common enemy" strategy. "I've called to help you understand the workers' comp system, since I'm not sure how good a job our adjusters do on this. Please let me know if you have any problem receiving your indemnity checks or have any other problems."

Measuring Success

The WCC can measure successful communication by the employee's attitude toward visits, calls, and letters. If the employee never comes on-site, routinely blocks telephone calls, refuses to collect certified mail, and never responds to letters, the WCC has not succeeded in keeping the channels of communication open. If this is due to poor communication techniques and not due to an employee intent on fraud, the WCC should improve his or her techniques by having someone listen in or observe and make suggestions. Sometimes a few sessions of role-playing, with a co-worker acting as a disgruntled employee, will improve the WCC's communication skills.

Source of Further Information

Fisher R, Ury W, Patton B. *Getting to Yes: Negotiating Agreement Without Giving In.* New York, Penguin Books, 1991.

Form 18-1, Guidelines for Communicating with Injured or Ill Employees

Purpose of Form

- To serve the workers' comp coordinator (WCC) as a quick summary of effective communication techniques, with examples
- To establish what the tone of calls to employees should be

Use of Form

- Put the form in a notebook reserved for open cases.
- Refer to it prior to making calls to employees.
- Use it for role-playing practices.
- Edit it to make it site-specific.
- Add to it sentences or approaches that have been particularly effective or well received.

Form 18-1

GUIDELINES FOR COMMUNICATING WITH INJURED OR ILL EMPLOYEES

To ensure active listening, take steps to prevent all interruptions. Prior to calling, determine what the main objective is: establishing a trusting relationship, finding out information, imparting information, or some other purpose? Write down the goal of the call and keep the goal in front of you.

Begin in a friendly way, express concern, and state the purpose of the call early on to reduce the recipient's anxiety. Avoid questions that can be answered with a "yes" or "no."

WCC: "Hello,___[employee name]___. This is _[your name]_. I'm calling from [the company, school, plant, shop, store, yard, head office, etc.] to find out how you're doing. I'm so sorry about your accident. How are you feeling now?"

Encourage the employee to talk about *feelings*. Elicit feelings through mirroring or repeating one or two words that the employee has used; this is sometimes called the "reflective technique."

Employee: "Well, the doc says I'm on the mend, but you never know."

WCC: "Never know?"

Another technique is to restate feelings to see whether the listener is understanding them correctly. This gives the appearance of agreeing without really doing so.

Employee: "You know how it is. They never play it straight with you."

WCC: "You sound worried that the doctor hasn't told you everything."

Employee: "You bet I am. If all I've got is back strain, how come my legs hurt?"

The WCC should be alert for an opportunity to play advocate for the employee by running interference with the insurer or the health-care provider. (Many employees are afraid to question physicians and become frustrated when dealing with large bureaucracies like insurers.) The WCC's assistance may help the employee view the WCC as "on my side."

WCC: "I wish I could answer that for you. Why don't I ask the doctor to call you to clear this up?"

Try to get the employee in a "yes" frame of mind. Positive answers help to foster optimism and confidence.

Employee: "O.K. Go ahead and try that."

WCC: "That's terrific. Is it all right if I call you in a few days to find out how everything is?"

Employee: "Sure. You know where to look for me!"

19

Case Management

Once a work injury or illness occurs, the choice is clear: Manage the process or be prepared to see large sums of money spent unnecessarily. If the employer fails to manage a case, the employee may receive inappropriate medical care, may be put completely out of work when able to perform modified duty, may become angry with a noncommunicative employer, may seek an attorney sooner rather than later, may wind up with permanent disability when rehabilitation was possible, and may cost the company a sizeable sum when the case may have warranted only a small expenditure.

Practical tip If an employee falls from a 12-story building, the time to start planning rehabilitation is when she or he passes the 11th-floor window. The goal of case management is to assist employees in reaching the highest medical improvement possible and returning to work.

Don't leave case management to the insurance adjuster! Adjusters are buried under hundreds of claims and usually have no financial incentive to reduce the costs of the claim or return the employee to work at the earliest possible date. After all, if an employer's workers' comp losses go from bad to worse, the insurance carrier just raises the organization's premium the next year to recoup the costs. Unfortunately, it's not so easy for the organization, if for profit, to pass such increases on to its customers or, if not for profit, to obtain additional funding.

Responsibilities of the Workers' Comp Coordinator

As described in Chapter 6, the ideal workers' comp coordinator (WCC) is a nurse familiar with the company's jobs and modified-duty program. If it is not possible to employ a nurse, the next logical choice for WCC is someone with a caring attitude and interest in rehabilitating injured or ill workers. *The WCC should be notified immediately of every on-the-job injury or illness.* The WCC should begin to manage the claim from the moment of the loss. The WCC should first ensure that the injured employee is directed to the preferred health-care provider, if possible, or other appropriate care. The WCC's main responsibilities are summarized below; keys to loss control are subsequently described. The **Case Tracker** (Form 19-1) is invaluable to the WCC in managing cases and fulfilling his or her responsibilities.

The WCC's main responsibilities are:

- Reviewing the compensability of the claim.
- Ensuring that the accident has been investigated.
- Maintaining contact with employees with work-related injuries or illnesses.
- Acting as advocate for employees with work-related injuries and illnesses, when appropriate.
- Reviewing medical care and response to treatment.
- Expediting treatment.
- Filing all required forms. Many insurers prefer to be notified of losses immediately rather than after a certain number of lost work days have elapsed, which is often what triggers reporting to the state workers' comp agency. Although some employers prefer to pay small claims directly, it is always wise to notify the insurance carrier in case a seemingly small claim later turns into a much larger loss. Even if the WCC has doubts about the compensability of a claim, he or she should nevertheless report it if the employee alleges work-relatedness.
- Reviewing medical bills prior to their submission to the insurance carrier. Make sure that no charges for treatment of unrelated conditions are included—that is, exercise vigilance for the "while-y'er syndrome," as in, "While y'er at it, could you remove these three moles?" In addition, keep in mind that workers' comp medical coverage is intended to return the employee to his or her level of functioning immediately prior to the work-related injury or illness, not to a higher level.

Example An employee with arthritis of the left hip fell in an icy parking lot at work and fractured a bone in his left leg. The treating physician wished to repair the fracture surgically and, at the same time, perform an artificial hip replacement to treat a preexisting condition. Workers' comp insurance covered only the procedure to fix the fractured leg bone.

- Keeping statistics on days lost, days of modified duty, number of litigated cases, and medical and indemnity costs per case. These statistics help to evaluate how successful case management has been and indicate where the WCC should focus future efforts.
- Attending safety committee meetings to "put a human and financial face on" the meaning of the accident to the company and to the worker. Often, safety committees are unaware of the potentially immense cost of even "minor" accidents.

Example A worker at a wire manufacturer reported several times to a safety-committee representative that a passageway door was sticking, causing him to open it by leaning into it with his shoulder. No action was taken until he dislocated his shoulder in this maneuver. The door was promptly planed down—a $24 repair job.

What the company's safety committee did not learn until 16 months later was that the injury proved to be career-ending for this 38-year-old laborer, who had to undergo several surgical procedures and never returned to work. The company's insurance carrier paid out thousands in medical and indemnity payments and was negotiating a lump-sum settlement for permanent disability. Once the safety committee learned of the extent of the loss from the newly appointed WCC, it began to attend to problems at the complaint stage rather than after they produced a loss.

Keys to Loss Control

Reviewing Compensability

The WCC should review claims and accident investigation reports to assess compensability, that is, whether the injury or illness qualifies for workers' comp. The WCC should advise the insurer if he or she is in doubt about compensability.

1. *Did the personal injury or illness arise out of, and in the course of, employment?* Did the injury or illness occur during work hours but while the employee was off the work premises on a personal errand? Did the injury or illness occur at work but not relate to duties?

Example An employee from a temporary-employment agency was assigned to a production facility. An hour after reporting for work, he began to have seizures and was taken to the nearest hospital's emergency department. The diagnosis was acute alcohol and drug withdrawal. The employee claimed that his illness was covered by workers' comp because it happened at work. After reviewing the medical findings, the insurance adjuster denied payment. The employee did not pursue the claim.

Unwitnessed Monday-morning injuries deserve special attention, since there may be cost-shifting of accidents that occurred over the weekend, particularly when an employee has exhausted sick time or health-insurance benefits. In addition, consider whether the reported accident or condition was sufficient or likely to produce the injury.

Example A teacher of people with developmental disabilities reported to her supervisor that she was having surgery for carpal tunnel syndrome in 2 weeks and that her condition was work related. She requested that a workers' comp claim be filed with the insurer, since she was planning on receiving indemnity payments during her 6-week convalescence. She had been wearing a wrist splint for 2 months but had never mentioned work-relatedness. An occupational health nurse reviewed the employee's job activities and found that none involved repetitive motion of the wrist. In addition, the nurse contacted the treating physician and found out that the employee had had this condition for several years prior to employment. She recommended that the insurer deny the claim. The employee had surgery but did not pursue the claim.

2. *Did the employee file the claim within the time period allowed by the statute of limitations?* Most workers' comp laws state that employees have a limited time period to make claims. The clock begins to run when the employee knew or should have known about the injury or loss of function. Consider whether the claim presented falls within this time period, as specified in state law.

Maintaining Contact with Employees

TALE OF TWO ACCIDENTS

Tale 1 It's Monday morning. News is traveling through the shop about Pete, who was in an automobile accident Saturday night. He is hospitalized following surgery for several fractures. A group of co-workers takes up a collection and sends flowers and a get-well card. A few co-workers go to visit him after work.

Tale 2 It's Monday morning. News is traveling through the shop about Fred, who fell off the plant's loading dock Sunday night and is hospitalized for a fractured hip. One employee jokes, "He should have watched that first step—it's a doozy." Others grumble about the accident costing this month's safety bonus. No card, no flowers, no visit. Why the different response?

These are examples of events that too often occur in the workplace. Those injured on the job are often ignored or forgotten by co-workers, in sharp contrast to those who are hurt off the job. In cases like that described in Tale 2, sympathy is too often replaced with blame, causing injured employees to become resentful and alienated and thus reducing their motivation to return to work.

Employees who are berated for causing the accident by not following safety procedures or who are repeatedly asked when they are returning to work will soon learn to take their phone off the hook or otherwise avoid answering calls. The WCC should make every effort to keep relations friendly and helpful and maintain regular contact with the employee. When communication from the employer becomes accusatory or ceases, many injured or ill workers seek attorneys for solace and protection, a turn of events that will usually lengthen the claim and make it more costly. *If an employee does retain a lawyer, the WCC should check state law to see whether it is legal to continue contacting the employee directly without prior approval from the attorney.*

If permitted, the WCC should contact an employee with a work-related injury or illness within 24 to 48 hours of the lost-time accident to express concern, to explain when to expect the first check from the insurer, to describe the availability of modified duty, and to describe his/her role and function as WCC.

Practical tip Consider sending a get-well card or flowers if the injury or illness is severe or will result in extensive lost work time. Some employers arrange to cover wages (until the employee begins to receive compensation checks) with a written agreement that the employee will reimburse the company and that the company will restore any used sick leave. Include injured and ill employees in company functions, if possible, to keep them connected with peers. One company president even had his out-on-disability employees in for lunch once a month! It's not surprising that the number of days lost per injury began to decrease rapidly in that facility, probably due to a combination of the Sentinel Effect (someone watching) and the Hawthorne Effect[1] (showing attention and concern).

---

[1] Named for the New Jersey town where a 1925 factory study at first attributed a gain in productivity to improved lighting, when in fact the gain was attributable to the increased attention researchers paid to the workers.

If the employee is not a candidate for modified duty, the WCC should nevertheless maintain contact even after extended absences, until the case is closed. The calls may drop in frequency from weekly to monthly, but the WCC should maintain the link. In addition, the employee's supervisor should periodically call the employee to keep him or her informed about events at work and to express concern (but not to question length of disability or validity of the injury).

Employee Advocacy

A small percentage of employees with work-related injuries or illnesses will retain an attorney on the way to getting medical care. However, most won't obtain legal representation unless they feel "pushed into it" by perceived poor treatment by the employer, the insurance company, the health-care provider, or the workers' comp system. Once a lawyer is involved, the case becomes adversarial, communication breaks down, and chances for quick resolution are dimmed.

The WCC has an opportunity to prevent this battle line from being drawn by being empathetic and acting on the employee's behalf. The WCC can address employee's concerns as soon as they are expressed. For example, if an insurer has not sent indemnity checks as required, the WCC should find out why. After all, the insurance company or third-party administrator is the company's agent.

If the employee dislikes the preferred health-care provider or feels that he or she is not receiving adequate medical care, the WCC can intervene by presenting the concerns to the health-care provider for an explanation. In some states, workers' compensation treatment protocols prohibit certain services until a specific number of days have elapsed following the injury or illness—for example, magnetic resonance imaging (MRI) may not be permitted until the employee has had 2 weeks of continuing symptoms. Once the WCC explains the reasons for the current treatment plan, most employees will understand that they are not being undertreated. In so-called *employee-choice states*, the WCC can advise injured employees that they have the right to switch to another provider, within the limits of the law.

The WCC should be aware of services the insurer has available to injured employees, such as rehabilitation nurses, and request their services when necessary. These services are included in the insurance premium.

It is better to acknowledge the feelings of disgruntled employees than to dispute them. Try simple statements like, "I'm sorry you're upset. Let me look into this problem." This approach is more likely to win cooperation than declarations like, "You're wrong. They mailed your check 2 weeks ago."

If the injured employee begins to see the WCC as helpful and not simply "management's mouthpiece," most injured employees will resolve their claims and come back to work without ever hiring a lawyer. This is the best result for everyone (except the lawyers).

Obtaining Second Medical Opinions or Independent Medical Examinations

If a case seems to drag on with little progress, if there is a question as to whether the injury or illness was caused by employment, or if the treating health-care provider does not release the injured or ill employee for modified duty despite apparent recovery, the WCC should arrange for a second medical opinion or independent medical examination (IME), particularly if the treating health-care provider is not the one designated by the company. Most workers' comp laws require an injured or ill employee to agree to additional examinations by health-care providers chosen by either the insurer or employer. The employee's refusal can be grounds for termination of benefits. The WCC can arrange this exam directly or ask the insurance adjuster to refer the employee. Reassure the injured or ill employee that the purpose of the second opinion is to be certain that the employee is obtaining the best medical care and treatment possible.

These exams are called *independent medical exams (IMEs)* when used by the insurer to resolve medical issues relating to the claim, such as degree of impairment or work capacity. They are called *second medical opinions* when the goal is assessment of the appropriateness of treatment or length of disability.

A second opinion is always appropriate when the treating physician has recommended surgery. In addition, referral to another physician often benefits injured or ill employees by giving them access to specialists. Ask the employee to bring along all medical records, radiographs ("x-rays"), and other test results. Send a copy of the accident description and the description of essential physical functions needed to perform the injured or ill employee's job. The employer should ask that the examiner address specific questions, such as the appropriateness of current treatment or work restrictions.

> **Example** When a clerical employee of a medical-instrument maker was scheduled for a surgical release of carpal tunnel ligaments 2 weeks after numbness and tingling appeared in her right hand, the WCC referred her to an occupational health specialist for a second opinion regarding the advisability of surgery. This physician confirmed the diagnosis but recommended that the employee postpone surgery for an 8-week trial of conservative treatment, including night splints, modified duty, job redesign, and occupational therapy. At the end of this time, she was sufficiently encouraged by her recovery to cancel her surgical plans.

The WCC should compile a list of health-care providers who understand the treatment of occupational injuries and illnesses and are willing to provide second opinions. Many providers are reluctant to accept workers' comp claims because of slow payment, low reimbursement rates, the possibility of having to testify in court, and the lengthened recovery time of many industrially injured patients.

The WCC should make an extra effort to reduce paper work and red tape for cooperative health-care providers. Send fill-in-the-blank letters and contact them only when necessary and only after allowing sufficient time for them to gather and review information on the injured employee. Learn who their receptionists are and treat them with unfailing courtesy. In short, make the experience as pleasant and brief as possible.

Some employers retain consulting physicians to whom they refer *all* injured employees for second medical opinions. Although this has certain advantages, those opinions are perceived by almost everyone as biased in favor of the company, which dilutes their authority.

Reviewing Length of Disability

The WCC should question long periods of disability that appear out of proportion to the injury or treatment. Here are some red flags:

- Employee ordered out of work for a month or longer without any intervening medical treatment or follow-up visits.
- Reports of employee being seen participating in activities inconsistent with the alleged extent of incapacity to work.

The WCC can ask the company nurse or doctor, if any, whether certain lengths of disability are reasonable. If the company does not have a nurse or doctor on staff or retainer, the WCC can use a published guide on disability duration (see "Sources of Further Information" at the end of this chapter).

Expediting Treatment

Many employees are put out of work needlessly while they wait for diagnostic tests or for appointments with busy specialists. If the WCC learns that the next medical evaluation is on hold while awaiting completion of tests or consultations, the WCC should try to shorten these delays by seeking alternate arrangements.

Example An employee of a temporary-employment agency reported wrist pain that disabled her for her assembly job. The treating physician referred her to a neurologist, with an appointment 6 weeks hence. The WCC obtained the name of a less busy neurologist with an opening in 1 week. On the basis of that exam, which was negative, the employee was cleared to return to a transitional assignment (modified duty).

Contacting Insurance Adjusters

The WCC should contact the insurance adjuster as soon as possible after filing a claim to discuss the circumstances of the injury or illness, concerns about compensability, and plans for managing the case. The WCC should advise the adjuster if the prospects are good for returning the injured or ill employee to work. Often this communication will help to keep estimates of potential financial losses lower than if the adjuster assumes a "worst case" scenario based on past experience with employees with the same diagnosis— for example, back strain. If an employee returns to work in full- or modified-duty capacity, notify the adjuster immediately to stop or modify indemnity payments.

An adjuster usually manages 200-300 cases by following standard insurer protocols. Therefore, the adjuster is rarely able to apply individualized or innovative approaches to reducing the severity of a claim. It is up to the WCC to suggest these approaches.

> **Example** A construction worker reported an unwitnessed injury to his back. He sought treatment from a chiropractor who declared him completely unable to work due to a diagnosis of herniated disc. The insurance company's doctor agreed with the chiropractor's opinion of his work status, based on the employee's continuing complaints of severe pain months after the alleged incident. The employee refused a neurosurgical consult and rejected modified-duty offers, citing the recommendation of his health-care provider. The adjuster's protocol called for an investigator to conduct an activity check after 9 months of total disability. However, the WCC learned after 5 months that the injured employee had an early-morning newspaper delivery route and requested an earlier investigation. When the employee's job activities were documented by the insurer on videotape, his benefits were terminated.

Reviewing Fee-Schedule Compliance

Many states publish a fee schedule that prescribes a maximum amount for medical services. Ask the insurer if it audits its bills for fee-schedule compliance. If not, the WCC can obtain a copy of the schedule and conduct periodic reviews to prevent overpayment of medical claims. Self-insurers often hire outside bill auditors to perform this service.

Reviewing Treatment-Protocol Compliance

Certain states now limit the type and frequency of medical treatments by diagnosis and length of time since the injury or illness. However, some insurers have been slow to review workers' comp claims for compliance with these protocols. The WCC can provide this review, sometimes identifying health-care services (type or frequency) that have been delivered but are not covered, thereby saving money on the claim.

Obtaining Periodic Loss Runs

Another tool for controlling costs is asking the insurer for periodic loss runs. These statistics summarize the cost of cases over several years and include current status. If the WCC is keeping a running total of company-paid sick days and medical bills for workers' comp cases, he or she can compare these numbers with the loss run to ensure that expenses have not been wrongly allocated, paid in duplicate, or paid in excess of the fee schedule for that service.

In addition, loss runs include information on *reserves*, which are the insurer's prediction of how much the case is going to cost before it's settled. The reserve figures are submitted yearly to the insurance rating bureau and have a profound effect on the size of the company's premium for the following year. The WCC should work vigorously to reduce any unreasonable reserves and to settle open claims as soon as possible.

Making Modified-Duty (Transitional Work) Assignments

The single most effective way to reduce the cost of workers' comp cases is to bring injured or ill workers back to work in some capacity as soon as possible. These assignments should be temporary and support treatment goals.

In some cases, health-care providers are reluctant to approve modified duty. It may be necessary for the WCC to accompany the employee when he or she visits the health-care provider and ask for a joint consultation at the end of the provider's examination. The WCC should bring a written description of the proposed modified-duty assignment and state that when the employee is ready to return to work in any capacity, the WCC will guarantee full compliance with work restrictions and with the treatment plan. This personal visit often sways reluctant health-care providers in favor of modified duty.

Recommending Rehabilitation Services

Some employees may not be able to return to their previous jobs due to loss of function or medical recommendations. Most workers' comp laws provide for vocational rehabilitation. The WCC should know what services and benefits are offered and suggest that the injured employee take advantage of them. The lowest-cost solution is for the employee to be retrained for a job at the original employer. However, if this is not possible, vocational rehabilitation will often restore at least partial earning capacity to an injured employee and hence reduce the size of the ultimate settlement.

Sources of Further Information

Fleeson WP. *Going on Comp: How to Get Through a Workers' Compensation Injury Without Losing Your Cool.* Duluth, MN, Med-Ed Books, 1991.

Reed P. *The Medical Disability Advisor: Workplace Guidelines for Disability Duration* (2nd ed). Denver, Reed Group, 1994.

Form 19-1, Case Tracker

Purpose of the Form

- As a guide to standard case management practices that are effective in hastening the back-to-work process
- To keep track of progress and highlight stumbling blocks
- As a reminder of important filing dates and other activities
- To keep communication open in a supportive and nonpunitive way
- To document employee responses to job offers and assistance, for use in possible litigation or settlement

Use of the Form

- Three-hole punch the form and put it in an "Open Cases" notebook.
- Enter the injured or ill employee's name on a Case Tracker form and immediately fill out dates, based on the date of the incident (DOI) and statutory reporting requirements.
- Review weekly the Case Tracker for meeting reporting requirements and other case-management milestones.
- As each scheduled action is completed, note the date.
- On the back of the form, note results of actions. For example, an entry for the first contact with an injured or ill employee might read:

  4/2/93, 2 p.m.: Called J.W. at home to express concern over his injury, to offer sick pay until indemnity checks begin, and to reassure him that we are available to assist in his recovery. Explained the claims process and our modified-duty policy. Employee had many questions about whether we will hold job open until he returns.

- In the event of settlement negotiations or litigation, provide a copy of the Case Tracker to the insurance adjuster or attorney.

Form 19 - 1
CASE TRACKER

Employee Name: _____ Date of Accident: _____

ID # _____ Home Tel.: _____

WEEK 1:

ACTION	Scheduled	Completed
1. Obtain completed Medical Treatment Report (Form 16-2).	DOI	
2. Obtain completed Accident Report.	DOI	
3. Contact employee.	DOI	
4. Review work restrictions with supervisor.	DOI	
5. Make temporary modified-duty offer (if medically cleared); if not medically cleared, advise health-care professional of available modified-duty assignments.	DOI	
6. Next medical appointment with:		
7. Record on OSHA 200 and 101 or equivalent (if recordable).	DOI + 6 workdays	
8. Send card or flowers, if appropriate.		
9. File forms with insurer, state, employee according to state/insurer requirements.	DOI + days	
10.		

* DOI = Date of Incident

WEEK 2:

ACTION	Scheduled	Completed
1. Contact employee.	DOI + 7	
2. Verify employee kept follow-up medical appointment.	Date of #6 above	
3. Obtain follow-up Medical Treatment Report.	Date of #6 above	
4. Next medical appointment with:		
5. Discuss case with claim adjuster, particularly early resolution.	DOI + 8	
6. Offer temporary modified duty (if medically cleared); if not medically cleared, advise health-care professional of available modified-duty assignments.	DOI + 7	
7. If not medically cleared, ask provider for estimated return-to-work date.		
8.		
9.		
10.		

Workers' Comp Management from A to Z: A "How to" Guide with Forms. © Nancy Nivison Menzel, OEM Press, Beverly, MA, 1994.

WEEK 3:

ACTION	Scheduled	Completed
1. Contact employee.	DOI + 14	
2. Verify employee kept follow-up medical appointment.	Date of #4 above	
3. Obtain follow-up Medical Treatment Report and review restrictions.	Date of #4 above	
4. Next medical appointment with:		
5. Schedule second opinion (if employee not returned to work).	DOI + 14	
6. Offer temporary modified duty (if medically cleared); if not medically cleared, advise health-care professional of available modified-duty assignments.	DOI + 14	
7. If on modified duty, review appropriateness.		
8.		
9.		
10.		

WEEK 4:

ACTION	Scheduled	Completed
1. Contact employee.	DOI + 21	
2. Verify employee kept follow-up medical appointment.	Date of #4 above	
3. Obtain follow-up Medical Treatment Report.	Date of #4 above	
4. Next medical appointment with:		
5. If on modified duty, review restrictions for progress and assignment for suitability.	DOI + 21	
6. Discuss modified duty assignments with supervisor.	DOI + 21	
7. Offer temporary modified duty (if medically cleared); if not medically cleared, advise health-care professional of available modified-duty assignments.	DOI + 21	
8. Discuss work status, reserves, IME, rehabilitation plan, case closure with adjuster.	DOI + 21	
9.		
10.		

Workers' Comp Management from A to Z: A "How to" Guide with Forms. © Nancy Nivison Menzel, OEM Press, Beverly, MA, 1994.

Form 19-1, Page 2

WEEK 5:

ACTION	Scheduled	Completed
1. Contact employee.	DOI + 28	
2. Verify employee kept follow-up medical appointment.	Date of #4 above	
3. Obtain follow-up Medical Treatment Report.	Date of #4 above	
4. Next medical appointment with:		
5. Offer temporary modified duty (if medically cleared); if not medically cleared, advise health-care professional of available modified-duty assignments.	DOI + 28	
6. Request loss runs from insurer.	DOI + 28	
7.		
8.		
9.		
10.		

WEEK 6:

ACTION	Scheduled	Completed
1. Contact employee.	DOI + 35	
2. Verify employee kept follow-up medical appointment.	Date of #4 above	
3. Obtain follow-up Medical Treatment Report.	Date of #4 above	
4. Next medical appointment with:		
5. Re-evaluate work status/modified-duty assignment.	DOI + 35	
6. Compare medical bills submitted with medical bills paid/allowed.	DOI + 35	
7. Compare insurer's indemnity payments with work days lost.	DOI + 35	
8. Review case with adjuster re. closure/settlement.		
9.		
10.		

SUBSEQUENT WEEKS

WEEK ___ :

ACTION	Scheduled	Completed
1. Contact employee.		
2. Verify employee kept follow-up medical appointment.		
3. Obtain follow-up Medical Treatment Report.		
4. Next medical appointment with:		
5. Re-evaluate work status/modified duty-assignment.		
6. Review case with adjuster re. closure/settlement.		
7.		
8.		
9.		
10.		

WEEK ___ :

ACTION	Scheduled	Completed
1. Contact employee.		
2. Verify employee kept follow-up medical appointment.		
3. Obtain follow-up Medical Treatment Report.		
4. Next medical appointment with:		
5. Re-evaluate work status/modified duty-assignment.		
6. Review case with adjuster re. closure/settlement.		
7.		
8.		
9.		
10.		

Workers' Comp Management from A to Z: A "How to" Guide with Forms. © Nancy Nivison Menzel, OEM Press, Beverly, MA, 1994.

20

Recognizing and Combatting Fraud, Abuse, and Malingering

John A. Davis, MD, and Nancy Nivison Menzel, MS, RN, COHN

The words "workers' compensation" often conjure up an unpleasant association with fraud and deception. One workers' comp manager reported he had become so cynical that his first question after an accident was "Were there any witnesses?" and not "How is the employee?" While there is sometimes truth behind the perception that many compensation claims are spurious or inflated, a few bad experiences sometimes prejudice case and claim managers against many workers with legitimate work-related injuries or illnesses. It is important for employers to be able to differentiate between these workers and those who would abuse the system for personal gain.

What Is Fraud?

Fraud is knowingly making false or misleading claims or statements about an accident or injury for financial gain. This includes claims for accidents or injuries that never occurred or didn't happen at work. In many states, the element of intention to mislead must be present for the action to be considered fraud. However, intention is difficult to prove. Estimates of the amount of fraud vary from 5% to 25% of workers' comp cases.

Exaggerated claims appear more widespread than intentional fraud. Abuse of workers' comp benefits exists on a continuum from malingering, in which the employee may exaggerate the extent of a disability to gain more days off or a higher financial settlement, to outright fraud, such as collecting workers' comp payments while employed elsewhere. Often, the persistent complaint of ongoing pain by the claimant is the only basis for sustaining disability. Unfortunately, there are no objective criteria for confirming the validity of reported pain.

Sometimes claims are exaggerated by incorrectly associating functional impairment with disability. Physical impairment is an anatomic or pathologic abnormality leading to loss of a normal body ability; for example, a carpenter with a crushed thumb may be unable to bend it. The assessment of impairment is based on objective structural limitations and is solely a medical responsibility. Disability, on the other hand, is the diminished capacity for everyday activities and gainful employment and is based largely on the injured or ill employee's subjective report. The carpenter may report that her crushed thumb makes it impossible for her to grasp a hammer, affecting employment. Ultimately, however, disability ratings and compensation awards are an administrative or legal, not medical, responsibility and are based on both the claimant's report of disability and the health-care provider's assessment of physical impairment.

Who Is Involved?

In addition to dishonest employees, some health-care providers abuse the system by extending an employee's time away from work beyond what the particular injury or illness requires, falsely certifying that an injury or illness was work-related to gain 100% reimbursement for medical bills, or ordering unnecessary tests and therapies to run up the bill. Health-care providers may also inappropriately interpret diagnostic tests by exaggerating the importance of either abnormal or variant findings or by misrepresenting preexisting abnormalities as being related to the current disability claim.

Some attorneys promote malingering by advising claimants to conceal signs of recovery to ensure a higher lump sum settlement, among other abuses. It is not unusual to see injured or ill workers undergo dramatic post-settlement improvement when there is no longer anything to gain by remaining disabled.

Some employers commit fraud by providing false information on payroll classifications to get a lower rate or by failing to report workplace injuries to avoid increases in the experience modification factor.

Why Is the System Abused?

The causes of fraud and abuse are complex. They include:

- Resentment toward the employer

- Incorrect belief that the money comes from the insurance company (and not ultimately from the employer)
- Employee's feeling of entitlement to compensation benefits
- Other employees bragging about receiving benefits for nonexistent or exaggerated symptoms
- The ease of deception without detection
- Cost-shifting from general disability insurance, which does not pay wage-replacement benefits, to workers' comp coverage
- Dishonesty
- Inadequate investigation of claims

In settings in which workers' comp is repeatedly abused or defrauded by employees without consequence, many other employees may be tempted to file false claims. Managers must carefully examine the circumstances of all claims to counteract abuse.

Example A long-time employee reported on a Monday morning that she had slipped on ice in the parking lot and that she had hurt her back. There were no witnesses. She said she felt well enough to drive to her physician's office, which was nearby. She later called in to say she had been put on bed rest for a few days.

The company had recently hired a contract case manager who called the employee to inquire about her condition. The employee became defensive and challenged the case manager by saying, "Why are you calling me at home? I'm not like some of them. I work hard, and I've earned a few days off." The case manager reassured her that she was interested in helping her and would call the next day to assess recovery.

When the case manager called again, the phone was busy all day. The physician's office advised the case manager that the employee had originally been seen in an emergency room for an injury she had sustained at home over the weekend. The insurer subsequently denied the claim.

Workers' comp medical coverage is usually 100%, whereas medical insurance often covers only 80%. In addition, workers' comp covers wage replacement, whereas time off for other injuries is covered only if the employer offers paid sick leave. This promotes cost-shifting from one type of coverage to the other.

Companies that do not offer medical insurance sometimes experience extensive cost-shifting. To get medical care for a nonoccupational injury, employees simply state that it happened at work.

Example An auto-parts manufacturer was experiencing a very high frequency of workers' comp claims. It did not offer health insurance until an employee had been with the company for 6 months. To try to reduce the frequency of claims, the company hired a nurse for 1 day a week to give on-site primary care and provide referrals, while shortening eligibility for health insurance to 6 weeks. As a result, the frequency of workers' comp claims dropped abruptly.

When Does the Most Abuse and Fraud Occur?

Some employees file false or exaggerated claims just before a layoff or before being fired. One reason is that workers' compensation benefits usually last longer than unemployment benefits. If your company is planning on downsizing or has seasonal workers, scrutinize all compensation claims submitted in the period 3 months prior to the layoffs.

Other employees may file false claims as retaliation against the employer, his or her supervisor, or a co-worker. The time to deal with personnel problems is before they become comp problems. Once disgruntled employees are off the job on workers' comp, it is a daunting task to get them to return.

Other employees may intentionally extend their disability in response to a sense that they have been ignored, forgotten, or treated harshly. It is the manager's job to identify and address these grievances long before they cause delays in rehabilitating an injured or ill employee.

Some employees intent on workers' comp fraud may take a job just to be able to file a claim. This type of employee typically reports an accident within the first 30 days of employment and sometimes sooner.

Example A car-repair shop hired a mechanic who stated on the second day of employment that he had hurt his back when lifting a tire. He went to a chiropractor, who certified that he was totally unable to work due to disability. An independent medical exam reported few physical findings, but the employee complained of great pain. The injured employee hired a lawyer, who negotiated a lump-sum settlement from the insurer, which chose not to dispute the claim. The employer found out subsequently that this employee had collected on a similar workers' comp claim against a previous employer.

What Settings Are High Risk for Abuse and Fraud?

Certain workplaces are more subject to abuse of workers' comp than others. One factor is whether the employer guarantees full wages to those injured on the job, as is common in some public entities like state governments. With wage-replacement insurance policies, the employee may receive more money by staying home than by working—a strong incentive to claim falsely or to delay recovery.

In other settings in which management takes no interest in managing cases or suffers no consequences (directly) for a high frequency of accidents, false or exaggerated comp claims can soar due to lack of scrutiny. Other employers, such as many police and fire departments, insist that an injured worker be 100% recovered before returning to duty. This requirement may promote symptom exaggeration to prolong the length of paid absence.

Finally, fraud is observed more often in certain states than in others. California, Florida, and Massachusetts have set up special anti-fraud units to address the problem. Other states are likely to follow as fraud becomes more noticeable.

Recognizing "Medical Build-Up" or Abuse

Many factors can occur either independently or interactively to contribute to "medical build-up," a term for abuse of a workers' comp claim that captures the role of health-care providers. This abuse can be perpetrated by injured or ill employees who report symptoms beyond what would be expected (symptom magnification) or assume the sick role (illness behavior) or by health-care providers who order improper tests, misinterpret test results, or continue inappropriate or ineffective treatment.

Interpretation of Diagnostic Testing

A common means of medical build-up is for the health-care provider to either misinterpret abnormalities of testing or to exaggerate the significance of abnormal or variations of normal findings. Often, health-care providers fail to acknowledge that asymptomatic people may have abnormal diagnostic studies, including abnormal findings of magnetic resonance imaging (MRI) and CAT scans, which may influence both recommended treatment and ultimate recovery. The most striking example is medical literature that details the fact that over 50% of women between the ages of 20-40 have asymptomatic abnormalities of the lumbar (lower back) discs, including bulges and herniations. There are similar findings for the cervical spine (neck). Of people over the age of 50, approximately 90% have degenerative joint disease.

Furthermore, assessment of test results is dependent on the timing of the study in relationship to the reported injury. For instance, identification of a nerve root abnormality by electromyelography (EMG) and nerve conduction studies within the first 5 or 6 weeks of an injury may indicate a *preexisting* condition, since it generally takes a minimum of 6 weeks for a *new* injury to result in abnormalities in test results. Therefore, in complex cases, it is imperative that all medical testing and test results are reviewed in detail by a consulting medical team.

Appropriateness of Diagnostic Testing and Treatment

Several state jurisdictions have developed treatment guidelines for specific diagnoses. In 1993, Massachusetts promulgated guidelines for 25 diagnoses. Several of these treatment guidelines were abstracted from existing guidelines developed either by other states or organizations such as the American Academy of Orthopedics. One unique treatment guideline was that which was developed for assessment of soft tissue injuries of the back and neck. Within the protocol are not only specific recommendations regarding appropriateness of diagnostic testing but also specific recommendations regarding allowed modalities of treatment, such as physical therapy sessions and chiropractic treatment. As existing treatment guidelines are refined and new treatment guidelines are developed and adopted by more jurisdictions, the result should be more uniformity in treatment and earlier identification of health-care providers who abuse the system by administering excessive tests and treatment. In addition, these guidelines should result in earlier recognition of patients with characteristics of chronic pain syndrome.

Chronic Pain Syndrome

Sometimes injured employees react to their injuries and associated pain outside the bounds of what is considered normal or usual. There may be no conscious intent to deceive in this overreaction, which can take the form of an intense response to relatively minor injuries or prolonged perception of pain long after normal healing should have occurred. This syndrome is sometimes called "*chronic pain syndrome*," as opposed to "*symptom exaggeration*," which implies an intention to deceive. "*Symptom magnification*" is a term often used to describe seemingly unwarranted reactions to an injury or illness and is one component of chronic pain syndrome.

Employees who respond out of proportion to their injuries or illnesses may do so for complex physical and psychological reasons. Chronic pain is located in the same part of the brain as fear, anxiety, frustration, anger, and depression, making resolution of this problem difficult. Employers need to recognize the complexity of dealing with injured or ill employees with chronic pain syndrome and the difficulties involved in disengaging them from this difficult-to-resolve condition.

Identifying employees with the characteristics of chronic pain should allow an employer to understand that ongoing medical intervention in regard to both diagnostic testing and treatment may be counterproductive. When chronic pain behavior is fully operational, less medical intervention in the case is often more effective (to say nothing of less expensive or less frustrating) than stepping up the type and variety of medical testing and treatment.

Eight diagnostic characteristics ("the 8Ds") of chronic pain have been described in the American Medical Association's *Guides to the Evaluation of Permanent Impairment*, to assist the health-care provider in making a presumptive diagnosis of chronic pain syndrome. These include:

1. *Duration.* In the past, chronic pain was applied to pain of greater than 6 months' duration. However, recent research in workers' comp indicates that chronic pain characteristics can appear within the first week or two of a claim. This makes prompt recognition and identification of chronic pain critical for successful management.

2. *Dramatization.* Patients with chronic pain display unusual verbal and nonverbal pain behavior. Words used to describe the pain are emotionally charged, affective, and exaggerated. The patient may exhibit maladaptive, theatrical behavior, such as moaning, groaning, gasping, grimacing, posturing, or pantomiming. In addition, patients with chronic pain behavior will often become indignant and quite upset if the evaluating physician questions the validity of the pain response.

3. *Diagnostic dilemma.* Patients with chronic pain tend to have extensive histories of evaluations by multiple physicians. They have undergone repeated diagnostic studies, despite which the clinical impressions tend to be vague, inconsistent, and inaccurate.

4. *Drugs.* Patients with chronic pain are willing recipients of multiple drugs, and substance dependence and abuse are a frequent condition.

5. *Dependence.* Chronic pain patients not only become dependent on their physicians and make demands for excessive medical care but also develop dependency on their spouses and families.

6. *Depression.* The condition of chronic pain is characterized by emotional upheaval. Psychological test results generally indicate depression, hypochondriasis, and hysteria. Unhappiness, depression, despair, apprehension, irritability, and hostility become prevalent. Coping mechanisms are severely impaired. Low self-esteem results in increased dependence on others.

7. *Disuse.* Patients with chronic pain will pick up on their health-care provider's advice to be "cautious" and to avoid activities that will

increase their pain. The result is further self-imposed limitations in activity and the development of generalized deconditioning.

8. *Dysfunction.* Having lost adequate coping skills, patients with chronic pain begin to withdraw from the social milieu. They disengage from work, tend to alienate friends and family, and become increasingly isolated, eventually restricting their activities to the bare essentials of life. This further contributes to the patient's sense of total and complete disability.

Once a competent medical management team has identified an employee with chronic pain syndrome, the employer should pursue administrative resolution of the claim. The challenge for employers is to be able to differentiate the employee with chronic pain syndrome from an employee with a legitimate work-related injury or illness who may have a prolonged disability but is actively pursuing recovery.

What Can a Workers' Comp Coordinator Do?

- Review all claims by counting **"Red Flags" for Fraud** (Form 20-1). The "Sentinel Effect" of someone watching often results in fewer fraudulent claims and less malingering.

- Find out if your state or insurance company has an anti-fraud unit and report suspected cases. In some states, employers can sue employees for fraud. Consult with an attorney to find out if this would be a worthwhile approach in certain circumstances.

- Post your state's statute on workers' compensation fraud along with a notice that your company plans to report all such cases.

- Act quickly on obvious cases. (One employer spotted a newspaper photo of an employee out on complete disability due to a back injury who had the misfortune of winning a bowling tournament. The employer sent the photo and a letter to the employee's physician and the state's fraud bureau, which successfully pursued the case.)

- Make it clear to employees that those who file falsely are hurting honest workers by taking wage increases away from them and are *not* hurting the insurer.

- Encourage employees to report evidence of abuse. (One worker brought in a videotape of a supposedly back-injured employee water skiing.)

- Collect names and telephone numbers of accident witnesses.
- Deal with disciplinary and other personnel problems before they become workers' comp cases.
- Refer complex cases to a medical case management team that understands the complexities of not only the workers' comp system but also the various components that might contribute to medical build-up or exaggeration of a claim, including symptom magnification or chronic pain behavior by the claimant, misinterpretation and misuse of diagnostic testing and, last, inappropriate treatment.
- Carefully review claims of work-related stress and try to convince the insurer to contest them if they seem unwarranted by the facts.
- Contact the company's insurer to find out how it handles suspected cases of fraud. Ask what procedures it has in place to review claims for elements of fraud.
- Ask the insurer to investigate all cases of suspected fraud. The insurance adjuster will often assign an investigator to follow up on reports of second jobs or exaggerated symptoms. Some employers hire their own investigators, although their reports have no authority over how the claim is managed by the insurer. However, they sometimes uncover information that will influence the insurer to step up its own investigation.
- Make sure the company sets a good example by adhering to all insurance rules itself. This includes such things as reporting all accidents and correctly classifying payrolls.

Source of Further Information

American Medical Association. *Guides to the Evaluation of Permanent Impairment* (4th ed). Chicago, IL, American Medical Association, 1993.

Form 20-1, "Red Flags" for Fraud

Purpose of the Form

- To serve as a checklist for reviewing claims for fraud
- To put employees on notice that management is watching
- To notify the insurer of suspect claims

Use of Form

- Post a copy of the form on the employees' bulletin board, along with a copy of the sections of the workers' comp law that prohibit fraud and management's statement about reporting suspected fraud.
- Review all claims with this checklist in hand.
- Submit summaries of ''red flags'' on questionable cases to the insurer.

Form 20-1

"RED FLAGS" FOR FRAUD

1.	Was there an unexplained delay in reporting the injury?	Y
2.	Did the injury occur on a Monday morning or in an area that is not the employee's usual department?	Y
3.	Was the injury unwitnessed?	Y
4.	Has the employee changed the accident description?	Y
5.	Did the injury occur before a layoff or after another job action, like poor performance review?	Y
6.	Does the employee have a history of claiming workers' compensation injuries?	Y
7.	Did the employee not get along with co-workers?	Y
8.	Does the company have trouble reaching the employee at home?	Y
9.	Did the employee retain a lawyer before a doctor?	Y
10.	Is the employee using a health-care provider or lawyer with a reputation for handling questionable cases?	Y
11.	Has the employee refused or avoided tests or procedures that will confirm the injury or extent of disability?	Y
12.	Did the employee change health-care providers after being cleared to return to work?	Y
13.	Does the employee have relatives on compensation?	Y
14.	Have other employees questioned the accident?	Y
15.	Has the employee used up all sick and vacation time?	Y
16.	Is workers' compensation insurance the only type of medical insurance the employee has?	Y
17.	Is this a new employee (hired within last month)?	Y
18.	Does the injured worker list a post-office box as an address or can be contacted only through a friend or relative?	Y

TOTAL **YES** ANSWERS: _____

Any claim with more than three "yes" answers may involve fraud.

Workers' Comp Management from A to Z: A "How to" Guide with Forms. © Nancy Nivison Menzel, OEM Press, Beverly, MA, 1994.

21

Using Loss Runs To Control Claim Costs

Consider the building that your insurance carrier occupies. If you've never seen it, make a mental note of another carrier's building that you might have driven by. Chances are it is large, newly built, and situated in a desirable area. Now consider your own employment facility. Is there a difference? Why?

One reason is that insurers use a variety of business methods to avoid losing money, methods that minimize risks to the carrier. For example, the system of experience rating penalizes clients with bad experience and rewards those with good experience through a multiplier on premiums.

The *experience modification factor* is based (in part) on the amount of money that the insurance carrier estimates all open claims will cost before they are closed; these are called *reserves* (or *incurred amounts*). This estimate is added to the amount of money already paid out on the claim, the *paid amounts*. These totals are submitted annually to the organization that calculates the experience modification factor—either the National Council on Compensation Insurance (NCCI) or an individual state bureau. The higher the projected cost of cases, the higher the experience modification factor and the higher the premium will be. Thus, the actual and projected cost of a claim has a direct influence on the amount of premium an employer pays.

This effect is felt for a 3-year period in most states, after which the insurer is not recovering money for that claim from the insured party through higher premiums. (Some states allow the claim's cost to have an influence for 5 years under special circumstances.)

Reserves and paid amounts are submitted on unit statistical cards (see Chapter 3) to the rating organization 6 months after the policy expires and annually thereafter until the claim is no longer eligible for inclusion in the experience modification calculation. Once these claim costs have been submitted, it is not possible (in many states) to change them that year if the reserves are later lowered or eliminated, which is why employers should work toward lowering reserves and controlling claim costs before these figures are used to calculate the experience modification factor.

Requesting Loss Runs

The workers' comp coordinator (WCC) should ask the insurer, third-party administrator, or other claims manager to send a copy of the loss run quarterly. These loss runs may go by many different names, such as "claims activity listing," but all should contain particulars about the workers' comp claims, including the reserves that have been set for each claim. Loss runs also report the amount of money that has been paid to date for medical care, wage replacement, and administrative, legal, or miscellaneous expenses.

At first glance, loss runs may be difficult to interpret due to insurance jargon, medical terminology, or a confusing layout. In the sample loss run below, note that the rows have been stacked, making readability difficult.

	CLAIM ACTIVITY LISTING			DATE 02/05/94				
ACC DATE CLAIM NUMBER	OCCUPATION CLAIMANT NAME	RPT DATE		LOSS DESCRIPTION MEDICAL	INDEMNITY	EXPENSE	TOTAL RESERVES	PAID THIS PERIOD
5/26/93 67345XXWC123445	ASSEMBLER SMITH, MARY	6/17/93	RES PTD	*REPETITIVE MOTION CARPAL TUNNEL WRIST* 10,000.00 345.00	10,000.00 3,249.98	800.00 0.00	20,800.00 3,549.98	20.00
10/23/93 67323XXWC543211	OPERATOR JONES, WANDA	12/21/93	RES PTD	*REPEATED MOTION-CTS RT ARM* 5,000.00 288.55	5,000.00	400.00 3.30	10,400.00 291.85	291.85

Reviewing Loss Runs

These are the items that the WCC should review quarterly in loss runs:

- Do all the claims belong to the employer? Claims are sometimes posted to the wrong account.
- Is all information for each claim correct, logical, and up to date?

- Does the loss run show continuing indemnity payments for an employee who has returned to work?
- Has the claim been settled, yet the claim continues to appear on the loss run?
- Has indemnity been paid despite the fact that the employee has never missed work?
- If indemnity has been paid and the employee did miss work, does the sum shown accurately reflect the amount of lost time?

Example The WCC reviewed the loss runs and noted $3,000 of indemnity payments for an employee who had missed 3 weeks of work. The indemnity-benefit rate for the employee was $261 per week, so the indemnity payment should have been $783 (261 x 3). The WCC contacted the insurance adjuster about the $2,217 overpayment. The adjuster was unaware that the claimant had returned to work and consequently was continuing to pay benefits, which the employee accepted. The adjuster worked out a repayment schedule with the employee for the excess payment.

- Does the reserve for the claim seem reasonable in light of the nature of the injury or illness and extent of the disability?
- Do the amounts paid for medical care seem reasonable for the type of treatment received to date?
- What charges have been allocated to the "expense" or "other" category?

The WCC can use the **Cost Tracker and Strategy Worksheet** (Form 21-1) as an aid in reviewing loss runs. Figure 21-1 shows a sample of a completed worksheet.

How Case Reserves Are Set

Every carrier, third-party administrator, and self-insured administrator has its own system for estimating the costs of a claim before it is closed. Here are some of the factors that go into setting a dollar amount:

- Prospects for rehabilitation and recovery
- Estimated length of recuperation period
- Medical and legal costs in the state
- Nature and severity of the injury/illness
- Wage at time of injury/illness

- Type of work (e.g., heavy, moderate, light, sedentary, skilled, unskilled)
- Long-term effect of injury/illness on employee (loss of earning capacity, ability to be retrained, other skills)
- Employee's attitude toward employer and returning to work
- Employer's attitude toward accommodating employee
- Insurance adjuster's past experience with similar claims
- Insurance carrier's policies regarding reserves
- Whether the case is contested or controverted

Insurance adjusters follow certain guidelines and consider past experience and local costs when setting the reserve for a particular case. If an employee is out of work, the case contested, and the state liberal in awarding benefits to injured workers, look for the reserve on that claim to be higher than for a case with a similar diagnosis that is uncontested and with an established return-to-work date.

NAME *Claim Number*	D.O.I.	DIAGNOSIS	TREATMENT	WS	RESERVES This month Last month	ADJUSTER	PLAN	NOTES
Banks, Lou 123455667	6/12/93	repetitive motion R arm	medical visit	NW	$3,500.00 $0.00	N. Smallers	Review medical care	Call physician and supervisor
Stevens, Chrisy 987765562	8/12/93	tendinitis	wrist splint, NSAID		$4,000.00 $0.00	R. Parker	Physical Therapy	Call P. T.
Salerno, Ernest 987091234	12/31/92	Fx ribs	None current		$1,200.00 $1,200.00	A. Abile	Call adjuster in Aug.	Unit Stat Review in 3 months
Ivanel, Irene 896748392	9/18/92	CTS	Surgery L. 1/93	LTD	$52,000.00 $35,000.00	S. Mikes	Call adjuster q 3 wks.	Referred to rheumatologist by Dr. Spencer on 6/14/93
Lineman, Ralph 673645771	4/27/92	CTS bilateral	Surgery both	RTW	$30,000.00 $30,000.00	R. Parker	Reduce repetitive motion by job redesign	Have PT check that he takes exercise breaks
Elmont, Steve 987234675	10/14/87	back strain		LTD	$50,260.00 $50,260.00	J. Santoz		Case kept open to recover from second injury fund. Case does not impact current comp. premiums
Redbird, Bryan 978954432	11/19/92	RMD thumb; tenosynovitis R ring finger	Surgery in Feb. 93	NW	$20,800.00 $20,800.00	M. Helix	Call adjuster to advise of retirement	Has retired
Diaz, Juan 6738846932	1/1/93	back strain	No records	NW	$10,075.90 $5,000.00	R. Brown	Review hiring procedures	Adjuster has advised settlement. This was a new hire. Fraud?
Sampson, Melissa 675849303	3/26/93	ulnar nerve compression		F	$1,040.00 $0.00	J. Santoz	See if closed next run	Symptoms have disappeared with PT and desk change. Jay agreed to close case
Suchon, Vanya 673988285	2/1/93	overuse synd. hands; L lat epicondylitis	medical only	RD	$2,500.00 $5,000.00	J. Santoz	Treat conservatively	Report from 5/24/93 indicated improvement. Supervisor reports she states she is feeling better. Doctor revisit mid-Aug.
				SUMMARY	$175,375.90 $147,260.00		CHANGE 19.09%	

Fig. 21-1. Sample Cost Tracker and Strategy Worksheet

Negotiating Case Reserves

Insurance adjusters follow many cases and may not get updated information as often as the WCC does. The WCC should call the adjuster periodically to report any progress in the case, such as bringing the employee back in a modified-duty (transitional work) assignment.

Insurance adjusters are often willing to lower the reserve for a particular claim if given sufficient reason to do so. However, the WCC must first win the adjuster's trust by presenting a reasoned case and establishing a track record of correct assessment of probable case outcomes.

Example In the loss run shown on page 21-2 ("Claim Activity Listing"), note that the adjuster put an estimate of $10,400 on the reserve for Ms. Jones's case, although the employee had not missed any time (and thus was not entitled to any indemnity payments). The adjuster had set the reserve based on that particular company's history of employees claiming repetitive motion disorders, having surgery, and not returning to work. The WCC called the adjuster with the good news that the company had hired a physical therapist who had begun an on-site screening program to find cases early and provide intervention before symptoms worsened. The one medical bill for Ms. Jones's case was to obtain confirmation of the diagnosis prior to beginning an upper-extremity muscle-strengthening regimen. The WCC assured the adjuster that Ms. Jones's case had a very limited loss potential, since the employee was now much improved and had been reassigned to a less hand-intensive job. With these assurances from the WCC, the adjuster lowered the reserve to $5,000, with a promise to close the case completely if no bills for medical treatment were submitted or claims for indemnity made in the next 3 months.

Tracking Paid Amounts

Monitoring paid amounts, particularly those for indemnity and medical care, is also important in controlling the cost of a claim. If wage replacement costs are piling up, the WCC may be able to intervene by bringing the injured or ill employee back in a modified-duty capacity. If medical costs escalate every reporting period, the WCC can ask the insurance adjuster to suggest ways to reduce them, perhaps by reviewing whether the medical treatment being given continues to be effective or could be discontinued. If an intensive physical therapy program has become costly, perhaps the injured or ill employee can receive part of his or her work hardening in a suitably designed modified-duty job or at a health club instead of a physical therapy clinic. The WCC may find, through careful review of the charges, that they have been incorrectly posted to a claim, paid more than once, or paid in excess of what the state's fee schedule allows. In all cases, the WCC should closely monitor paid amounts.

The Most Important Factor

Does the injured employee have a job waiting? Employers who wish to keep claim costs (and their premiums) down should try to bring every injured employee back to work. Without strong prospects of a job for recovering workers, most insurance adjusters will be forced to set case reserves on the high side in anticipation of paying indemnity for a lengthy period, being held liable for costly medical bills, or having to offer a high lump-sum settlement because of the injured or ill worker's reduced earning capacity. The happiest outcome for everyone is successfully rehabilitating the injured or ill worker and gainfully employing him or her.

Source of Further Information

International Risk Management Institute. *The Workers' Compensation Guide.* Dallas, International Risk Management Institute, 1992. (To obtain this publication, call the institute at 800-827-4242.)

Form 21-1, Cost Tracker and Strategy Worksheet

Purpose of Form

- To track trends in reserves and paid amounts
- To serve as a reminder list for specific actions
- To serve as an "at a glance" overview of cases and quick reference
- To promote planning and claims management

Use of Form

- Request quarterly loss runs from the insurance carrier or administrator.
- Complete a new worksheet every month.
- Create the worksheet on a computer for easier manipulation of numbers, particularly when carrying over last month's figures, computing totals, and calculating percent differences between reporting periods.
- Compare amounts (reserves and paid) for individual cases and flag those that show unexpected increases.
- Total the amounts (reserves and paid) for all claims from one reporting period to the next. Compute the percent change by subtracting the smaller number from the larger one and dividing the resulting sum by last month's total. Indicate the direction of the change (up or down, plus or minus).

   Example Last month's total amount (reserves and paid): $50,000. Current month's total amount: $25,000. The difference is a decrease of $25,000, or 25,000 ÷ 50,000 = 50% decrease or a -50% change.)

- Analyze reasons for any increases and take appropriate action. For example, if the company total increased sharply due to many new cases, alert the safety committee about the problem.
- Note when the unit statistical review is scheduled (6 months after policy expiration) and work to control medical and indemnity costs and reduce reserves prior to that.
- Have the worksheet available when calling the insurance adjuster to allow ready access to the claim number and facts about case.
- Ask the insurance adjuster to review claim totals with you prior to submitting unit stat cards.

Form 21-1

COST TRACKER AND STRATEGY WORKSHEET

NAME Claim Number	D.O.I.	DIAGNOSIS	TREATMENT	W.S.	RESERVES This quarter Last quarter	PAID This quarter Last quarter	ADJUSTER	PLAN	NOTES

D.O.I.: date of injury

W.S.: work status

Workers' Comp Management from A to Z: A "How to" Guide with Forms. © Nancy Nivison Menzel, OEM Press, Beverly, MA, 1994.

22

Closing Cases

States administer workers' comp laws through a variety of means: courts, commissions, boards, or a combination of commissions and boards. Each state has laws and regulations that govern the process of making and settling claims, as well as resolving disputes.

The Employer's Best Approach

Companies should set, as a standard, avoiding legal disputes whenever possible through skillful case and claim management. The faster legitimate claims are closed, the less expensive they will be for all parties. The **ABC (Always Be Closing) Reminder List** (Form 22-1) is intended to aid the workers' comp coordinator (WCC) in expediting closures. However, whenever there is evidence of fraud, abuse, or attempts to set precedents, the company should be prepared to vigorously dispute any excessive or unwarranted awards. Ideally, claimants should be treated fairly, be paid their rightful compensation, and be returned to work. However, in the real world, things do not always work that way.

Reviewing an organization's past record points out whether any changes are needed in strategy. Employers should compare the number of claims they have had in the past 3 years that involved administrative hearings (and attorney involvement) with the number of claims that were settled or closed without resorting to litigation or dispute resolution.

If the company had many claims that it felt were groundless or exaggerated but few were challenged through the state's dispute resolution process, the insurer may be too quick to settle or may not have all the facts of the case when making a decision about contesting a claim. Word gets out to other employees of the company that a workers' comp claim can pay off faster than the state lottery. The employer should request a conference with the insurer or claims administrator to learn the reasons for this apparent ease of settling claims.

Employers who are not self-insured sign over to their insurers the right to decide whether to contest or settle claims. However, employers can make strong cases why certain claims should be disputed, by presenting facts about the circumstances surrounding the accident or co-workers' tips about the exaggerated nature of the injury, for example. Insurers want to please their clients. If the insurer settles too many dubious claims, the employer should consider this at policy-renewal time and shop around for another insurer, if in the voluntary market.

If the company has many apparently legitimate workers' comp claims that have become adversarial, the company must redress its safety record, its insurer's method of handling claims, or its treatment of injured workers. Injured or ill employees who have been alienated by unsafe work conditions or poor treatment by their employers or the insurer may seek revenge by dragging their claims through the administrative system.

To Settle or Contest?

Insurers have guidelines they follow regarding the cost of settling the claim versus the potential risk of pursuing the claim in court. This may result in settlements that seem to reward spurious or groundless claims but, in the long run, may save the employer money by lowering the ultimate payout or limiting similar claims.

Example After receiving several written warnings for excessive absenteeism, a production employee complained to the company's human resource department that the supervisor was prejudiced against him due to his race.

When the employee failed to report to work for a week without explanation, the supervisor fired him. The following day, the employee telephoned his supervisor and threatened to come to the plant with an assault rifle and kill him. The company had to hire guards and tighten security. By the end of the week, the employee had retained a lawyer and had filed a workers' comp claim, alleging stress and a work-related back injury. The insurer denied the claim for stress on the basis that the discharge had been a bona fide personnel action and denied the back injury claim because the employee had not reported an accident. When the employee contested this decision, however, the insurer chose to settle the claim for $10,000, due to fear of the potential "exposure" (high judgment costs) if it lost the stress claim at the hearing because of the employee's previous complaint of prejudice.

The insurer's decision to settle the claim may have been prudent, since it was a precedent-setting stress claim for that worksite. Had the insurer lost at the hearing, copy-cat claimants might decide to file for stress as well, creating an unexpected surge of cases that could be difficult to defend against after a judgment has been handed down.

Claims Resolution

For prolonged-recovery or permanent-disability cases that are not contested or not of questionable merit, insurers often try to *settle* (pay a lump sum of money to close) rather than continue paying complete- or partial-disability wage benefits over a long period of time. Settlement has advantages for both sides.

On the claimant's side, it allows injured or ill employees to go on with their lives, in some cases even *promoting* recovery because there is no longer anything to be gained from prolonged disability. Plaintiff attorneys often take workers' comp cases on a contingency basis, which means that they receive their fees as a percentage of the lump-sum settlement. Without a settlement, payment of their fee is delayed.

On the defendants' side, settlement allows employers and insurers to establish a substantially correct dollar figure for their loss, rather than trying to guess and plan for the cost of indemnity, rehabilitation, and litigation to be paid over many years into the future. (However, medical benefits may continue even after a claim has been settled.) Another cost-saving advantage of settlement is that it allows insurers to reduce their insurance adjusters' workloads by reducing the inventory of active claims, thereby reducing overhead and increasing productivity.

For employers, it is better to settle most claims, because once a claim is scheduled for litigation, insurers raise the case reserves, which adversely affects the employer's experience modification factor, thereby increasing insurance premiums. The employer's goal should be early resolution of all legitimate claims.

For a particular claim, insurance adjusters base settlement offers on a number of considerations, including:

- Nature and extent of injury
- Impairment rating from treating physician
- Impairment rating from the independent medical exam
- Fee schedule, if any, for impairment

- Preexisting conditions
- Present and future earning capacity, as affected by injury-related restrictions
- Age, education, transferable skills
- Length of time on job (2 weeks? 20 years?)
- Indications of fraud or malingering from surveillance (videotaping, observation, evidence of unreported employment)
- Degree of participation in rehabilitation services
- History of past workers' comp claims
- Need for, and value of, future medical care
- Any credits due, such as for overpayment of benefits or payment of unauthorized medical treatment
- Size of probable future benefits if not settled
- Willingness of employee/lawyer to settle
- Willingness of employer to settle
- Eagerness of insurer to settle

The settlement process is usually one of negotiation between the insurer and the injured or ill employee's lawyer, with each side presenting reasons for the dollar figure offered or requested. Either side may approach the other with a settlement offer, which the other party may accept, reject, or modify. The original offer from the insurance adjuster is usually at the low end and is designed to elicit an indication of interest from the injured employee. The process of offer/counteroffer continues until the parties reach an agreement or negotiations break down completely, whereupon the matter is settled through the state's workers' comp dispute-resolution process.

Employers should ask their insurers to advise them in advance of any proposed lump-sum settlements and to explain exactly how the insurance adjuster computed the figure. In some states, the employer must sign off on any final settlements. Ask the insurance carrier, agent, or adjuster whether the workers' comp law in your jurisdiction requires employer notification or approval.

Litigation Management

If employers/insurers and injured workers/lawyers can't reach a settlement agreement, the case enters the state's dispute-resolution process by either party formally seeking a binding decision from an independent third party. Employers sometimes speak of "winning" after a case has gone to dispute resolution. In reality, once a case is litigated, the employer has already lost money, productivity, management time, and probably the employee. Any third-party decision simply sets a "stop loss" on the amount.

Insurers' legal departments handle numerous claims, many of which they don't have time to review until a few days or hours prior to the hearing. Employers should work with the adjuster and the insurer's legal department to make certain they have all the facts of the case, including the company's efforts to rehabilitate an injured worker by providing appropriate modified duty and any "red flags" for fraud.

Attending the Proceedings

Employers should ask to be advised of the date and time of any hearings, conferences, conciliations, arbitrations, mediations, or other administrative proceedings and, if possible, attend them. Employers may not be able to testify at some proceedings, but they can brief the insurer's attorney. In some proceedings, employers can present their view of the facts of the case, such as evidence that the employee failed to cooperate with treatment or refused legitimate modified-duty job offers.

Workers' comp judges, commissions, or boards sometimes view the employer's presence as an indication that the job offer is sincere. If the judge finds that the employee is capable of earning some money after the injury or illness as a result of the job offer, any lump-sum settlement will be reduced by that amount, called an *"earning capacity."*

Employers should request that the adjuster notify them of any decisions or proposed settlements in contested cases.

> **Example** A school employee tore his achilles tendon in a charity basketball game played on a Sunday. He claimed it was work related, since the principal of the school had solicited volunteers for the game at a staff meeting during business hours. The insurer denied the claim, since the law in that state specifically exempted voluntary athletic activities from workers' comp coverage. When the employee appealed the decision on the grounds that he had not "volunteered" but had been pressured into signing up by the principal, the insurer advised the school to settle for the small amount the claimant's attorney had requested, to make the claim "go away." The school refused to settle to avoid establishing a precedent, even after the conciliator at a preliminary hearing didn't dismiss the claim. Ultimately, an administrative law judge found that the claim was not supported by the law and denied compensation.

Employers who attend hearings or other proceedings, such as Alternative Dispute Resolution (ADR), should try to maintain a calm and reasonable demeanor, regardless of how exasperating they may find the claimant's behavior. Workers' comp decisions are often biased toward injured or ill employees rather than insurers or employers, who are viewed as having more resources. There's no point in tipping the scales of justice even further by raging at the system, the judge, the lawyer, or the injured employee. Such displays of emotion may make the judge sympathize with the employee about his or her purported stressful work situation and are public-relations failures.

Form 22-1, ABC (Always Be Closing) Reminder List

Purpose of Form

- To focus the workers' comp coordinator's attention on resolution of claims
- To provide suggestions to hasten closure of claims

Use of Form

- Put the form inside the notebook where Case Trackers (see Form 19-1) are kept for open cases.
- Read the list of suggestions on the form prior to every contact with an insurance adjuster or injured or ill employee.
- Consider that early closure of claims may benefit all parties and may be the most humane way to allow claimants to go on with their lives.

Form 22-1

ABC (ALWAYS BE CLOSING) REMINDER LIST

The faster that legitimate cases are closed, the less expensive they will be. Avoid legal and medical "build up" through early resolution!

Have I encouraged the employee to accept a modified-duty assignment?

Have I spoken to the insurance adjuster or claims administrator enthusiastically about the employee and return-to-work possibilities?

Have I asked the adjuster about plans to close the case, including specific actions planned and time periods for achieving them?

Have I asked the adjuster to allow me to review settlement offers in advance?

Have I provided the adjuster with facts that may affect settlement?

- Knowledge of transferrable skills, if any

- Presence of preexisting conditions

- Location of any preplacement or periodic physical examinations

- Knowledge of previous workers' comp claims or recent accidents outside of work

- Any evidence of noncooperation with treatment, like missed appointments

- Length of employment

- Disability retirement options

- Employee's pre-injury attitude toward employer

Have I encouraged the employee's supervisor about return-to-work prospects?

Workers' Comp Management from A to Z: A "How to" Guide with Forms. © Nancy Nivison Menzel, OEM Press, Beverly, MA, 1994.

23

Charting Injury/Illness Incidence, Severity, and Lost-Workday Case Incidence Rates

The best way to bring the workers' comp insurance premium down is to prevent accidents. One way of determining the effectiveness of accident-prevention programs is to calculate the number of workplace injuries and illnesses as an incidence rate (number per 100 full-time workers). For purposes of this calculation, limiting the count of injuries and illnesses to those that are OSHA-recordable standardizes incidence rates. This rate is called the "OSHA incidence rate."

After accident prevention, the next best way to reduce the premium is to reduce the cost of those accidents that do occur. A large component of the cost of accidents is wage replacement for time away from work (indemnity benefits). The effectiveness of case management can be measured by computing the rate of days lost per 100 workers, sometimes called the severity rate.

OSHA Recordability

Not all employers are regulated by OSHA. Among those who are regulated, employers with certain Standard Industrial Classification (SIC) codes must record most workplace injuries and illnesses on a special form, the OSHA 200 Log and Summary of Occupational Injuries and Illnesses, referred to as simply the "OSHA Log." OSHA will ask to see this log when making an inspection of an employer's premises, as a way of evaluating workplace safety. Although having an OSHA Log is not a regulatory requirement of workers' comp laws, OSHA sometimes will review an organization's workers' comp claim records to make sure that no qualifying injuries or illnesses have been omitted from the log.

The following are considered recordable under OSHA requirements:

- Occupational deaths
- All occupational illnesses, whether or not they result in lost time or medical treatment
- Occupational injuries that result in loss of consciousness, restriction of work or motion, transfer to another job, or medical treatment beyond first aid.

Calculating the Injury/Illness Incidence Rate

You may calculate the OSHA incidence rate monthly, cumulatively, annually, or for any other time period. The formula for finding the OSHA incidence rate is:

$$\frac{\text{Number of OSHA-recordable injuries and illnesses} \times 200,000}{\text{Employee hours worked}} = \text{OSHA incidence rate}$$

To find the total number of hours worked for all employees, use payroll records for the designated time period (e.g., monthly, yearly). Do not include hours taken for vacation, sick time, or holidays, since employees are not at work (and thus not exposed) during these times. The above formula includes multiplication by 200,000 to standardize the rate for 100 employees working 40 hours per week, 50 weeks a year.

> **Example** A foundry had 12 OSHA-recordable injuries and illnesses over a period when its employees worked 127,796 hours. Its OSHA incidence rate is 12 x 200,000 ÷ 127,796, or 18.8 per 100 full-time employees.

Calculating the Lost-Workday Case Incidence Rate

Similarly, one can compute the lost-workday case incidence rate by counting only those injuries and illnesses that resulted in lost time or restricted work activity, whether consecutive or not: e.g., total lost-workday cases x 200,000 ÷ total hours worked.

Calculating the Severity Rate

By adding up the actual number of days away from work and days of restricted work activity and substituting this figure for the number of injuries and illnesses in the above formula, the number of lost workdays per 100 employees, which is called the "severity rate," can be calculated.

Example A human-services organization with 250 employees who had worked 450,000 hours had 20 injuries and illnesses that resulted in 100 lost workdays in 12 months. The severity rate is calculated as follows: $100 \times 200,000 \div 475,000 = 42.1$ lost workdays per 100 full-time employees.

Analyzing Results

Companies can make internal comparisons, such as statistics from this year or month compared to last year or month, to determine trends. (See Form 23-1, **Monthly Summary of OSHA Recordable Injuries and Illnesses**.) They can compare themselves against a national benchmark as well: the experience of other companies in the same Standard Industrial Classification (SIC). In the human-services example above, its severity rate of 42.1 compares favorably with the national severity rate of 61.2 in 1991 for SIC code 832 (individual and family services).

To find the national rate for the company's SIC code, refer to the U.S. Department of Labor's *Occupational Injuries and Illnesses in the United States by Industry*. The most recent edition (published annually in April) can be ordered by calling the U. S. Government Printing Office at (202) 783-3238.

Analyze results and graph them to show trends and comparisons. Look for trends from one year to the next or for any repetitive patterns, particularly if the graph shows dips or peaks associated with certain months or company activities, like seasonal layoffs.

Example In 1993, a landscaping company (Lupine Landscape [a fictitious company name]) took steps to reduce the number of its workplace injuries and illnesses. It was successful in most months, as shown by a decrease in the OSHA incidence rate. However, when 1993 figures were compared with 1992 figures by graph (see below), it was obvious that there were two peaks: one in late spring and one in late fall. In the spring, the company hired many inexperienced workers as the company geared up for the summer. In the fall, the company routinely laid off most of them. To address these possible contributing factors, the company added a 2-week training period for new hires and took steps to reduce the number of layoffs needed by expanding its business into winter work.

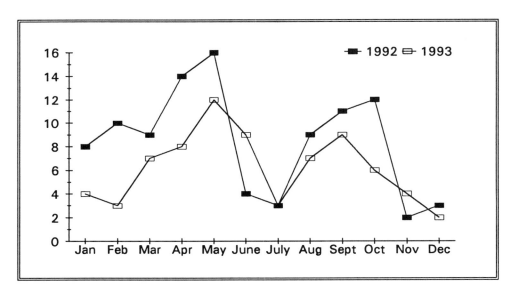

LUPINE LANDSCAPE'S OSHA INCIDENCE RATES

Sources of Further Information

U.S. Department of Labor, Bureau of Labor Statistics. *Recordkeeping Guidelines for Occupational Injuries and Illnesses.* Washington, DC, U.S. Government Printing Office, 1986.

U.S. Department of Labor, Bureau of Labor Statistics. *Occupational Injuries and Illnesses in the United States by Industry, 1991.* Washington, DC, U.S. Government Printing Office, 1993.

Form 23-1, Monthly Summary of OSHA-Recordable Injuries and Illnesses

Purpose of Form

- To track and compute OSHA incidence rates
- To analyze the effectiveness of safety programs and case-management activities in reducing incidence rates
- To highlight months with higher incidence rates

Use of Form

- The WCC should compute incidence rates for OSHA-recordable injuries and illnesses and lost workdays for that month, as well as keep a running, month-to-month cumulative total.
- The safety committee should review the results monthly.
- The results should be graphed by month, with the present year compared to previous years, as shown in the sample graph on Page 23-4.

Form 23-1

MONTHLY SUMMARY OF OSHA-RECORDABLE INJURIES AND ILLNESSES

COMPANY/LOCATION:

YEAR:

$$\text{INCIDENCE RATE} = \frac{\text{Total \# OSHA Recordable Cases or LWD} \times 200,000}{\text{Employee Hours Worked}}$$

PERIOD	Total Hours Worked	Fatals (A)	Lost Workday Cases (B)	Restricted WD Cases (C)	Medical Only Cases (D)	Total Cases (A+B+C+D)	Actual Lost/Restr. Workdays	OSHA Incidence Rate Inj./Ill.	OSHA Incidence Rate LWD
Jan.									
Feb.									
Cum.									
Mar.									
Cum.									
Apr.									
Cum.									
May									
Cum.									
June									
Cum.									
July									
Cum.									
Aug.									
Cum.									
Sept.									
Cum.									
Oct.									
Cum.									
Nov.									
Cum.									
Dec.									
YEAR									

Workers' Comp Management from A to Z: A "How to" Guide with Forms. © Nancy Nivison Menzel, OEM Press, Beverly, MA, 1994.

24

Evaluating Success of the Workers' Comp Management Program

When you get in a car for a journey, you establish your destination in advance. For example, "I am going to work" or "I am going to the movies." En route, you look for certain indications that confirm you are headed in the right direction and making progress in reaching your goal. Those markers may be road signs, landmarks, elapsed time, or odometer readings. If you have followed your planned course correctly, you will reach your destination.

The same logic applies to managing workers' comp. You must establish your goal in advance and periodically check your progress to make sure you are on course. If you begin to stray, you must correct your actions (or change your destination). Using the **Workers' Comp Management Effectiveness Analysis** (Form 24-1) will help you set goals and track progress.

Establishing Measurable Goals

First decide on your goal. What is reasonable in your circumstances? Striving to reduce the company's total insurance premium may be unrealistic if your company is expanding its work force or is located in a state where a large insurance-rate increase has just been approved.

However, it is appropriate to set as goals, *reductions in the OSHA incidence rate, severity rate,* or *lost-workday case incidence rates* (see Chapter 23). Meeting these goals translates into reduced human suffering and increased productivity, as well as reduced workers' comp and accident costs.

A company that last year experienced an incidence rate of 16 injuries/illnesses per 100 workers could set as a goal a 25% reduction for the next year to 12 injuries/illnesses per 100 workers. Similarly, companies that implement modified-duty programs should see a decrease in the severity rate (number of lost workdays per 100 employees). Management or the safety committee should select an appropriate percentage reduction as a target. Midyear calculations give an indication of progress toward achieving desired annual goals.

Another goal is reducing the *incurred loss percentage,* which is calculated by dividing the yearly total of incurred workers' comp losses (dollar amount) by total payroll for that year. These figures are found on the Experience Rating Calculation sheet, available from your workers' comp rating organization upon written request.

> **Example** An automobile service center had $252,252 in payroll in 1991, with $60,114 in incurred workers' comp losses; therefore, the incurred loss percentage was 24%. The following year, it implemented an active safety program and reduced its losses to $20,291 on a payroll of $202,308, for an incurred loss percentage of 10%, a significant improvement.

A very broad outcome indicator is the premium paid per employee. If your company currently pays $3,000 per employee, it might set as an ultimate target $500 per employee to be achieved through annual reductions of 20%. However, this figure is often a moving target, since premiums are affected by the rate set in the state, payroll classifications, and other factors not directly affected by the effectiveness of company safety and case-management programs. Nonetheless, the insurance premium paid per employee is an interesting statistic to track, provided that any trends are interpreted by considering extenuating circumstances.

Evaluating Outcomes

Reductions in the incidence of work-related injuries and illnesses, their severity, lost workdays, or the incurred loss percentage will produce a reduction in the experience modification factor, which will reduce premiums and associated penalties. This dollar savings will make the company stronger and more competitive. Some of the money saved should be directed toward strengthening the company's safety program.

If the company finds that loss trends are worsening, the safety program may be ineffective or there may be identifiable reasons, such as the initiation of an aggressive case-finding program for carpal tunnel syndrome. Management must analyze the reasons for the worsening trends and take immediate steps to reverse the situation, if possible. Has there been an increase in claims due to rumored layoffs? If so, there must be more rigorous investigation of claims and swift action to complete planned reductions in the work force. Are the supervisors sabotaging safety efforts? If so, they must bear the economic consequences through wage freezes and blocked promotions. Are claims rising due to a cause that is not addressed in the current safety program, such as repetitive motion injuries? Establish a task force to make recommendations for immediate loss-control measures.

Establishing Intangible Goals

Although it is important to use measurable results to determine the outcome of a company's workers' comp management program, there are other desirable outcomes to consider as well. Do the employees feel that the organization cares about their health and safety? Secure workers are happier and more productive than those worrying about their personal safety. Do clients and customers feel that the company incorporates safety? This enhances the company's quality image. Do banks and other financial institutions view the company as one with safe premises and fairly treated employees, which translates into their perception of the company as a good risk for loans and investments?

One way to find out public and employee perceptions of the company is to conduct satisfaction surveys. These can be quite revealing of employee opinions as well as of client viewpoints.

Practical tip Some companies are so proud of their safety records that they mount large signs in the parking lot that advertise the number of days without a lost time accident. This is both good public relations and a daily reminder to incoming employees.

There are no good reasons or valid excuses not to institute a total workers' comp management program in every workplace. Working safely increases efficiency and productivity. Safety programs reduce losses directly through accident prevention. Early-return-to-work programs reduce the costs associated with accidents, both in terms of human suffering and dollar losses. Private-sector employers who do not begin to institute these programs will find they become noncompetitive due to higher costs. Public entities will become subject to stricter outside regulation if they fail to control workers' comp costs themselves. Isn't today a good day to appoint a workers' comp coordinator and convene your safety committee?

Form 24-1, Workers' Comp Management Effectiveness Analysis

Purpose of Form

- To enable setting of goals for improvement in the workers' comp control program
- To encourage annual or semiannual review of the effectiveness of the safety and case-management programs
- To provide feedback to management about trends in the company's workers' comp control program and outcomes regarding established goals

Use of Form

- For each indicator, enter last year's results.
- Set a specific goal for reduction or improvement, either based on a percentage change or an actual number (e.g., incidence rate of 14/100 employees or less; 30% decrease in incurred loss percentage; 10% more employees responding affirmatively that this is a good place to work).
- Compute preliminary findings at midyear to estimate trends and intervene if necessary.

Form 24-1

WORKERS' COMP MANAGEMENT EFFECTIVENESS ANALYSIS

INDICATOR	LAST YEAR	GOAL (+,-,=)	THIS YEAR	PERCENT CHANGE
OSHA incidence rate				
Severity rate				
Lost-workday case incidence rate				
Incurred loss percentage				
Experience modification factor				
Premium per employee				
Employee satisfaction survey				

Workers' Comp Management from A to Z: A "How to" Guide with Forms. © Nancy Nivison Menzel, OEM Press, Beverly, MA, 1994.

APPENDIX A, SAMPLE LOSS-CONTROL REPORT

Run-of-the-Mill Fabric Company

XYZ Insurance Engineering Department

February 24, 1994

2-94-1   Fan

The blade guard on the fan located in the packing room does not meet OSHA requirements. All fans should have a guard with openings no greater than 1/2". This fan should either be discarded or a nylon-mesh guard installed over the existing one.

2-94-2   Lockers

Several of the lockers in the packing room are not secured and could easily fall and injure an employee.

2-94-3   Floor Holes

There are several holes in the floor where fabric was passed through but are no longer in use. These holes should be covered to keep employees from twisting an ankle or tripping.

2-94-4   Electrical

Several of the electrical cords on the lighting fixtures at the back end of the packing room appear to be damaged. These should be examined more closely and replaced if necessary.

The electrical panels at the back end of the packing room are blocked. These, and others, should be kept accessible at all times.

The exposed knife switch on the power panel in the generator room should be protected, so that employees cannot contact the live electrical parts. A simple barrier guard that will prevent employees from accidentally bumping the switch is all that is required.

2-94-5   Eye Washers

All eye-washer units should be equipped with dust caps to prevent the nozzles from getting clogged. The units should also be checked on a quarterly basis to ensure that they are working properly and to flush out the plumbing.

The location of the eye washers in the resin area should be marked with signs for easier identification. It is also necessary to install another unit closer to the tanks on the south side of the building.

2-94-6   Ladder

The fiber glass ladder located at the back end of the packing room is missing the top step. This needs to be repaired or the ladder discarded.

2-94-7 Hoists

OSHA regulations require that all cranes and hoists be visually checked on a monthly basis. I am enclosing a copy of a checklist for this purpose.

2-94-8 Resin Tanks

All resin tanks need to be labeled to comply with the OSHA hazard communication standard. This may be difficult, as tanks may contain different materials at various times. It may be necessary to incorporate the labeling with the job orders so that employees will have access to the appropriate information.

2-94-9 Respirators

If respirators are being used routinely, OSHA requires a written respirator program. I have enclosed a sample that can be adapted to suit your needs.

2-94-10 Platform #2 Resin Tanks

This platform is of concern because it is narrow, approximately 18" high, and without any rails. If an employee steps off the platform accidentally, he or she could suffer a severe injury. It is suggested that rails be installed along the back side of the platform.

2-94-11 Mixing Tanks

All mixing tanks should have lids to prevent chemicals from splashing out and vapors from escaping. The lids would also protect against accidental contact with moving blades or shafts.

If possible, the lids should be electrically interlocked so that the mixers cannot be operated if the lids are opened.

2-94-12 Noise

The noise from the compressed air release at the back end of the frame machines appears to be excessive. I realize that employees do not work in this area all the time, but it is an area that should be checked to determine the actual noise levels.

2-94-13 No. 4 Die Machine

The emergency stop buttons should be replaced with an emergency pull cord that will enable the machine to be stopped anywhere along its length.

2-94-14 Bag Handling

It is recommended that the size of the cartons that contain the bags of Glutex be cut to allow easier access to the bags. Currently, employees must bend into the box to pick up the bag, which is the position most likely to cause back injury. It is preferable for the employee to squat down as close to the bag and lift using his/her legs.

Appendix B, Directory of Approved Sources of OSHA-Funded Consultation

Alabama
7(c)(1) Onsite Consultation
  Program
Martha Parham West
P.O. Box 70388
Tuscaloosa, AL 35487
(205) 348-3033

Alaska
Division of Occupational
  Safety and Health
Alaska Department of Labor
3301 Eagle Street, Suite 303
Pouch 7-022
Anchorage, AK 99150
(907) 264-2688

Arizona
Consultation and Training
Division of Occupational Safety
  and Health
Industrial Commission of Arizona
800 West Washington
Phoenix, AZ 85007-9070
(602) 542-5795

Arkansas
OSHA Consultation
Arkansas Department of Labor
10421 West Markham
Little Rock, AK 72205
(501) 682-4522

California
CAL/OSHA Consultation Service
455 Golden Gate Avenue
Room 5246
San Francisco, CA 94102
(415) 703-4441

Colorado
Occupational Safety and Health
  Section
Institute of Rural Environmental
  Health
Colorado State University
110 Veterinary Science Building
Fort Collins, CO 80523
(303) 491-6151

Connecticut
Division of Occupational Safety
  and Health
Connecticut Department of Labor
200 Folly Brook Boulevard
Wethersfield, CT 06109
(203) 566-4550

Delaware
Occupational Safety and Health
Division of Industrial Affairs
Delaware Department of Labor
820 North French Street, 6th Floor
Wilmington, DE 19801
(302) 577-3908

District of Columbia
Office of Occupational Safety
  and Health
District of Columbia Department
  of Employment Services
950 Upshur Street, N.W.
Washington, DC 20011
(202) 576-6339

Florida
7(c)(1) Onsite Consultation
  Program
Bureau of Industrial Safety
  and Health
Department of Labor
  and Employment Security
2002 St. Augustine Road
Building E. Suite 45
Tallahassee, FL 32399-0633
(904) 488-3044

From U. S. Department of Labor, Occupational Safety and Health Administration. OSHA Handbook for Small Businesses, OSHA Publ. 2209, 1992 (Revised). Washington, DC, U. S. Government Printing Office.

Georgia
7(c)(1) Onsite Consultation
 Program
Georgia Institute of Technology
O'Keefe Building - Room 23
Atlanta, GA 30332
(404) 894-8274

Guam
OSHA Onsite Consultation
Government of Guam
Int'l Trade Center
3rd Floor
P.O. Box 9970
Tamuning, GU 96911
(671) 646-9244

Hawaii
Division of Occupational Safety
 and Health
830 Punchbowl Street
Honolulu, HI 96813
(808) 548-4155

Idaho
Safety and Health Consultation
 Program
Boise State University
Department of Commerce
 and Environmental Health
1910 University Drive, MG-110
Boise, ID 83725
(208) 385-3283

Illinois
Illinois Onsite Consultation
Industrial Services Division
Department of Commerce
 and Community Affairs
State of Illinois Center
100 West Randolph St.
Suite 3-400
Chicago, IL 60601
(312) 814-2337

Indiana
Division of Labor
Bureau of Safety, Education
 and Training
402 West Washington
Room W195
Indianapolis, IN 46204-2287
(317) 232-2688

Iowa
7(c)(1) Consultation Program
Iowa Bureau of Labor
1000 East Grand Avenue
Des Moines, IA 50319
(515) 281-5352

Kansas
Kansas 7(c)(1) Consultation
 Program
Kansas Department of Human
 Resources
512 West 6th Street
Topeka, KS 66603
(913) 296-4386

Kentucky
Division of Education and Training
Kentucky Labort Cabinet
U.S. Highway 127, South, 1049
Frankfort, KY 40601
(502) 564-6895

Louisiana
7(c)(1) Consultation Program
Office of Workers' Compensation
Louisiana Department of Labor
1001 North 23rd Street
Baton Rouge, LA 70804-9094
(504) 342-9601

Maine
Division of Industrial Safety
Maine Department of Labor
State Home Station 82
Hallowell Annex
Augusta, ME 04333
(207) 289-6460

Maryland
7(c)(1) Consultation Services
Division of Labor and Industry
501 Saint Paul Place
Baltimore, MD 21202
(301) 333-4218

Massachusetts
7(c)(1) Consultation Program
Division of Industrial Safety
Massachusetts Department
 of Labor and Industries
100 Cambridge Street
Boston, MA 02202
(617) 727-3463

Michigan
Michigan Department of Public Health
Division of Occupational Health
3423 N. Logan Street
P.O. Box 30195
Lansing, MI 48909
(517) 335-8250

Bureau of Safety and Regulation
Michigan Department of Labor
7150 Harris Drive
P.O. Box 30015
Lansing, MI 48909
(517) 322-1809

Minnesota
Consultation Division
Department of Labor and Industry
443 Lafayette Road
St. Paul, MN 55155
(612) 297-2393

Mississippi
7(c)(1) Onsite Consultation Program
Division of Occupational Safety
    and Health
Mississsippi State Board of Health
305 West Lorenz Boulevard
Jackson, MS 39219-1700
(601) 987-3981

Missouri
Onsite Consultation Program
Division of Labor Standards
Department of Labor and Industrial
    Relations
3315 West Truman Boulevard
Jefferson City, MO 65109
(314) 751-3403

Montana
Department of Labor and Industry
Employment Relations Division
Safety Bureau
Arcade Building, 111 North Main
Helena, MT 59604-8011
(406) 444-6401

Nebraska
Division of Safety, Labor and Safety
    Standards
Nebraska Department of Labor
State Office Building
301 Centennial Mall, South
Lincoln, NE 68509-5024
(402) 471-4717

Nevada
Preventive Safety
2500 W. Washington, Suite 104
Las Vegas, NV 89158
(702) 486-5016

New Hampshire
Onsite Consultation Program
New Hampshire Department
    of Labor
19 Pillsbury Street
Concord, NH 03301
(603) 271-2024

New Jersey
Division of Workplace Standards
New Jersey Department of Labor
CN386
Trenton, NJ 08625-0953
(609) 292-7036

New Mexico
OSHA Consultation
Occupational Health and Safety
    Bureau
1190 St. Francis Drive, Room N-2200
Santa Fe, NM 87504-0968
(505) 827-2885

New York
Division of Safety and Health
State Office Campus
Building 12, Room 457
Albany, NY 12240
(518) 457-2481

North Carolina
North Carolina Consultative
    Services
North Carolina Department
    of Labor
OSH Bureau of Consultative Services
413 North Salisbury Street
Raleigh, NC 27603
(919) 733-3949

North Dakota
Division of Environmental
    Engineering
North Dakota State Department
    of Health
1200 Missouri Avenue, Room 304
Bismarck, ND 58502-5520
(701) 221-5188

Ohio
Division of Onsite Consultation
Department of Industrial
  Relations
2323 West 5th Avenue
P.O. Box 825
Columbus, OH 43216
(614) 644-2631

Oklahoma
OSHA Division
Oklahoma Department of Labor
4001 North Lincoln Boulevard
Oklahoma City, OK 73105-5212
(405) 528-1500

Oregon
7(c)(1) Consultation Program
Department of Insurance
  and Finance/APD
Labor and Industries Building
Salem, OR 97310
(503) 378-3272

Pennsylvania
Indiana University of Pennsylvania
Safety Sciences Department
205 Uhler Hall
Indiana, PA 15705
(412) 357-2561/2396
(Toll free in state)
(800) 382-1241

Puerto Rico
Occupational Safety and Health
  Office
Puerto Rico Department of Labor
  and Human Resources
505 Munoz Rivera Avenue, 21st Floor
Hato Rey, PR 00918
(809) 754-2134/2171

Rhode Island
Division of Occupational Health
Rhode Island Department
  of Health
206 Cannon Building
75 Davis Street
Providence, RI 02908
(401) 277-2438

South Carolina
7(c)(1) Onsite Consultation
  Program
Consultation and Monitoring, SC
  DOL
3600 Forest Drive
P.O. Box 11329
Columbia, SC 29211
(803) 734-9599

South Dakota
S.T.A.T.E. Engineering Extension
Onsite Technical Division
South Dakota State University
PO Box 2218
Brookings, SD 57007
(605) 688-4101

Tennessee
OSHA Consultative Services
Tennessee Department of Labor
501 Union Building, 6th Floor
Nashville, TN 37219
(615) 741-7036

Texas
Texas Workers' Comp. Commission
Health & Safety Division
200 East Riverside Drive
Austin, TX 78704
(512) 440-3834

Utah
Utah Safety and Health
Consultation Service
160 East 300 South, 3rd Floor
Salt Lake City, UT 84151-0870
(801) 530-6868

Vermont
Division of Occupational Safety
  and Health
Vermont Department of Labor
  and Industry
118 State Street
Montpelier, VT 05602
(802) 828-2765

Virginia
Virginia Department of Labor
  and Industry
Voluntary Safety and Health Compliance
13 S. 13th Street
Richmond, VA 23219
(804) 786-6613

Virgin Islands
Division of Occupational Safety
   and Health
Virgin Islands Department of Labor
Lagoon Street
Frederiksted, VI 00840
(809) 772-1315

Washington
Voluntary Services
Washington Department of Labor
   and Industries
1011 Plum Street, M/S HC-462
Olympia, WA 98504
(206) 586-0963

West Virginia
West Virginia Department
   of Labor
State Capitol, Building 3,
   Room 319
1800 E. Washington Street
Charleston, WV 25305
(304) 348-7890

Wisconsin
Section of Occupational Health
Wisconsin Department of Health
   and Human Services
1414 E. Washington Avenue
   Room 112
Madison, WI 53703
(608) 266-8579

Wisconsin Department of Industry
   Labor and Human Relations
Bureau of Safety Inspection
401 Pilot Court, Suite C
Waukesha, WI 53188
(414) 521-5063

Wyoming
Occupational Health and Safety
State of Wyoming
122 West 25th, Herschler Bldg.
Cheyenne, WY 82002
(307) 777-7786

Appendix C, Local and Regional OSHA Offices

The following is a list of addresses and telephone numbers of OSHA Area Offices. These offices are sources of information, publications, and assistance in understanding the requirements of the standards.

They can furnish you the basic publications you need:

1. *Job Safety and Health Protection* (the OSHA workplace poster).

2. The OSHA recordkeeping requirements.

3. A copy of the appropriate set of standards.

4. A large selection of publications concerned with safe work practices, control of hazardous substances, employer and employee rights and responsibilities and other subjects.

Feel free to contact these offices by phone, by mail or in person, without fear of triggering an inspection. However, if you request OSHA compliance personnel to visit your place of business, they are required to issue citations if a violation of an OSHA standard is observed. (We suggest you request a consultation visit instead.)

ALABAMA
Birmingham, AL 35216
2047 Canyon Road-Todd Mall
Telephone: (205) 731-1534

Mobile, AL 36693
3737 Government Blvd.
Suite 100
Telephone: (205) 441-6131

ALASKA
Anchorage, AK 99513-7571
Federal Bldg., USCH Room 211
222 West 7th Ave., #29
Telephone: (907) 271-5152

ARIZONA
Phoenix, AZ 85016
3221 North 16th St-Suite 100
Telephone: (602) 640-2007

ARKANSAS
Little Rock, AR 72201
Savers Bldg., Suite 828
320 West Capitol Avenue
Telephone: (501) 324-6291

CALIFORNIA
San Francisco, CA 94105
71 Stevenson St.
Suite 415
Telephone: (415) 744-7120

COLORADO
Denver, CO 80204
1244 Speer Blvd.
Collonnade Center, Suite 360
Telephone: (303) 844-5285

Englewood, CO 80111
7935 E. Prentice Ave.
Suite 209
Telephone: (303) 843-4500

CONNECTICUT
Bridgeport, CT 06604
One Lafayette Square, Suite 202
Telephone: (203) 579-5579

Hartford, CT 06103
Federal Office Building
450 Main Street-Rm. 508
Telephone: (203) 240-3152

FLORIDA
Fort Lauderdale, FL 33324
Jacaranda Executive Court
8040 Peters Rd., Bldg. H-100
Telephone: (305) 424-0242

Jacksonville, FL 32216
3100 University Blvd., South
Telephone: (904) 232-2895

Tampa, FL 33610
5807 Breckenridge Parkway
Suite A
Telephone: (813) 626-1177

GEORGIA
Savannah, GA 31401
1600 Drayton Street
Telephone: (912) 944-4393

Smyrna, GA 30080
2400 Herodian Way, Suite 250
Telephone: (404) 984-8700

Tucker, GA 30084
Bldg. 7, Suite 110
La Vista Perimeter Office Park
Telephone: (404) 493-6644

HAWAII
Honolulu, HI 96850
300 Ala Moana Blvd.-Suite 5122
Telephone: (808) 541-2685

IDAHO
Boise, ID 83702
Suite 134
3050 North Lake Harbor Lane
Telephone: (208) 334-1867

ILLINOIS
Calumet City, IL 60409
1600 16th St.-Suite 12
Telephone: (708) 891-3800

From U. S. Department of Labor, Occupational Safety and Health Administration. OSHA Handbook for Small Businesses, OSHA Publ. 2209, 1992 (Revised). Washington, DC, U. S. Government Printing Office.

Des Plaines, IL 60018
2360 E. Devon Avenue
Suite 1010
Telephone: (708) 803-4800

North Aurora, IL 60542
344 Smoke Tree Business Park
Telephone: (708) 896-8700

Peoria, IL 61614-1223
2918 West Willow Knolls Rd.
Suite 101
Telephone: (309) 671-7033

INDIANA
Indianapolis, IN 46204
46 East Ohio Street-Rm. 423
Telephone: (317) 331-7290

IOWA
Des Moines, IA 50309
210 Walnut Street-Rm. 815
Telephone: (515) 284-4794

KANSAS
Wichita, KS 67202
216 N. Waco-Suite B
Telephone: (316) 269-6644

KENTUCKY
Frankfort, KY 40601
John C. Watts Fed. Bldg.-Rm. 108
330 W. Broadway
Telephone: (502) 227-7024

LOUISIANA
Baton Rouge, LA 70806
2156 Wooddale Blvd.
Hoover Annex-Suite 200
Telephone: (504) 389-0474

MAINE
Augusta, ME 04330
U.S. Federal Bldg.
40 Western Ave.-Rm. 121
Telephone: (207) 622-8417

MARYLAND
Baltimore, MD 21201
Federal Bldg.-Rm. 1110
Charles Center, 31 Hopkins Plaza
Telephone: (301) 962-2840

MASSACHUSETTS
Braintree, MA 02184
639 Granite Street
4th Floor
Telephone: (617) 565-6924

Methuen, MA 01844
Valley Office Park
13 Branch Street
Telephone: (617) 565-8110

Springfield, MA 01103-1493
1145 Main Street-Rm. 108
Telephone: (413) 785-0123

MICHIGAN
Lansing, MI 48917
801 South Waverly Rd.
Suite 306
Telephone: (517) 377-1892

MINNESOTA
Minneapolis, MN 55401
110 South 4th Street-Rm 425
Telephone: (612) 348-1994

MISSISSIPPI
Jackson, MS 39269
Federal Bldg.-Suite 1445
100 West Capitol Street
Telephone: (601) 965-4606

MISSOURI
Kansas City, MO 64106
6200 Connecticut Ave.
Suite 100
Telephone: (816) 483-9531

St. Louis, MO 63120
4300 Goodfellow Blvd.-Bldg. 105E
Telephone: (314) 263-2749

MONTANA
Billings, MT 59101
19 N. 25th Street
Telephone: (406) 657-6649

NEBRASKA
Omaha, NE 68106
Overland-Wolf Bldg.-Rm. 100
6910 Pacific Street
Telephone: (402) 221-3182

NEVADA
Carson City, NV 98701
1050 East Williams, Suite 435
Telephone: (702) 885-6963

NEW HAMPSHIRE
Concord, NH 03301
279 Pleasant Street
Suite 201
Telephone: (603) 225-1629

NEW JERSEY
Avenel, NJ 07001
Plaza 35-Suite 205
1030 Saint Georges Ave.
Telephone: (201) 750-3270

Hasbrouck Heights, NJ 07604
Teterboro Airport
Professional Bldg., 2nd Floor
500 Route 17 South
Telephone: (201) 288-1700

Marlton, NJ 08053
Marlton Executive Park
701 Route 73 South, Bldg. 2
Suite 120
Telephone: (609) 757-5181

Parsippany, NJ 07054
299 Cherry Hill Road
Telephone: (201) 263-1003

NEW MEXICO
Albuquerque, NM 87102
320 Central Ave., S.W.
Suite 5613
Telephone: (505) 776-3411

NEW YORK
Albany, NY 12205-3826
401 New Karner Road, Suite 300
Telephone: (518) 472-2468

Bayside, NY 11361
42-40 Bell Blvd. 5th Floor
Telephone: (718) 279-9060

Bowmansville, NY 14026
5360 Genesee Street
Telephone: (716) 684-3891

New York, NY 10007
90 Church Street-Rm. 1407
Telephone: (212) 264-9840

Syracuse, NY 13260
100 S. Clinton Street-Rm. 1267
Telephone: (315) 423-5188

Tarrytown, NY 10591
660 White Plains Road
4th Floor
Telephone: (914) 683-9530

Westbury, NY 11590
990 Westbury Rd.
Telephone: (516) 334-3344

NORTH CAROLINA
Raleigh, NC 27601
Century Station-Rm. 104
300 Fayetteville Street Mall
Telephone: (919) 856-4770

NORTH DAKOTA
Bismarck, ND 58501
Federal Bldg.-Rm 348
PO Box 2439
Telephone: (701) 250-4521

OHIO
Cincinnati, OH 45246
36 Triangle Park Drive
Telephone: (513) 841-4132

Cleveland, OH 44199
Federal Office Bldg.-Rm. 899
1240 East Ninth Street
Telephone: (216) 522-3818

Columbus, OH 43215
Federal Office Bldg.-Rm. 620
200 N. High Street
Telephone: (614) 469-5582

Toledo, OH 43604
Federal Office Bldg.-Rm. 734
234 North Summit Street
Telephone: (419) 259-7542

OKLAHOMA
Oklahoma City, OK 73102
420 West Main Place-Suite 725
Telephone: (405) 231-5351

OREGON
Portland, OR 97204
1220 S.W. Third Ave.-Rm. 640
Telephone: (503) 326-2251

PENNSYLVANIA
Allentown, PA 18102
850 N. 5th Street
Telephone: (215) 776-0592

Erie, PA 16506
Suite B-12
3939 West Ridge Road
Telephone: (814) 453-4351

Harrisburg, PA 17109
Progress Plaza
49 N. Progress Street
Telephone: (717) 782-3902

Philadelphia, PA 19106
U.S. Custom House-Rm. 242
Second and Chestnut Street
Telephone: (215) 597-4955

Pittsburgh, PA 15222
Federal Bldg.-Room 1428
1000 Liberty Ave.-Rm. 2236
Telephone: (412) 644-2903

Wilkes-Barre, PA 18701
Penn Place-Rm. 2005
20 North Pennsylvania Ave.
Telephone: (717) 826-6538

PUERTO RICO
Hato Rey, PR 00918
U.S. Courthouse & FOB
Carlos Chardon St.-Room 559
Telephone: (809) 766-5457

RHODE ISLAND
Providence, RI 02903
380 Westminster Mall
Room 243
Telephone: (401) 528-4669

SOUTH CAROLINA
Columbia, SC 29201
1835 Assembly Street
Rm. 1468
Telephone: (803) 765-5904

TENNESSEE
Nashville, TN 37215
2002 Richard Jones Rd.
Suite C-205
Telephone: (615) 736-5313

TEXAS
Austin, TX 78701
611 East 6th Street-Rm. 303
Telephone: (512) 482-5783

Corpus Christi, TX 78401
Government Plaza-Rm. 300
400 Mann Street
Telephone: (512) 888-3257

Dallas, TX 75228
8344 East R.L. Thornton Freeway
Suite 420
Telephone: (214) 320-2400

Fort Worth, TX 76180-7604
North Star 2 Bldg.
Suite 430
8713 Airport Freeway
Telephone: (817) 885-7025

Houston, TX 77060
350 North Sam Houston Pkwy.,
Suite 120
Telephone: (713) 591-2438

Houston, TX 77004
2320 La Branch Street-Room 1103
Telephone: (713) 750-1727

Lubbock, TX 79401
Federal Bldg.-Rm. 421
1205 Texas Avenue
Telephone: (806) 743-7681

UTAH
Salt Lake City, UT 84165-0200
1781 South 300 West
Telephone: (801) 524-5080

VIRGINIA
Norfolk, VA 23510
FOB, Rm. 835
200 Granby Mall
Mall Drawer 486
Telephone: (804) 441-3820

WASHINGTON
BELLEVUE, WA 98004
121 107th Ave N.E.
Telephone: (206) 553-7520

WEST VIRGINIA
Charleston, WV 25301
550 Eagan Street-Rm. 206
Telephone: (304) 347-5937

WISCONSIN
Appleton, WI 54915
2618 North Ballard Road
Telephone: (414) 734-4521

Madison, WI 53716
4802 East Broadway
Telephone: (608) 264-5388

Milwaukee, WI 53203
Suite 1180
310 West Wisconsin Ave.
Telephone: (414) 291-3315

OSHA Regional Offices

If you are unable to contact your local OSHA Area Office, you may contact the appropriate OSHA Regional Office for information and/or assistance.

Region I
(CT,* MA, ME, NH, RI, VT*)
133 Portland Street
1st Floor
Boston, MA 02114
Telephone: (617) 565-7164

Region II
(NJ, NY,* PR,* VI*)
201 Varick Street
Room 670
New York, NY 10014
Telephone: (212) 337-2378

Region III
(DC, DE, MD,* PA, VA,* WV)
Gateway Building, Suite 2100
3535 Market Street
Philadelphia, PA 19104
Telephone: (215) 596-1201

Region IV
(AL, FL, GA, KY,* MS, NC,*
SC,* TN*)
1375 Peachtree Street, N.E.
Suite 587
Atlanta, GA 30367
Telephone: (404) 347-3573

Region V
(IL, IN,* MI,* MN,* OH, WI)
230 South Dearborn Street
Room 3244
Chicago, IL 60604
Telephone: (312) 353-2220

Region VI
(AR, LA, NM,* OK, TX)
525 Griffin Street
Room 602
Dallas, TX 75202
Telephone: (214) 767-4731

Region VII
(IA,* KS, MO, NE)
911 Walnut Street
Room 406
Kansas City, MO 64106
Telephone: (816) 426-5861

Region VIII
(CO, MT, ND, SD, UT,* WY*)
Federal Building, Room 1576
1961 Stout Street
Denver, CO 80294
Telephone: (303) 844-3061

Region IX
(American Samoa, AZ,* CA,* Guam,
HI,* NV,* Trust Territories of the Pacific)
71 Stevenson Street
Room 415
San Francisco, CA 94105
Telephone: (415) 744-6670

Region X
(AK,* ID, OR,* WA*)
1111 Third Avenue, Suite 715
Seattle, WA 98101-3212
Telephone: (206) 553-5930

*These states and territories operate their own OSHA-approved job safety and health programs (Connecticut and New York plans cover public employees only). States with approved programs must have a standard that is identical to, or at least as effective as, the federal standard.